ARSHILE GORKY

The Breakthrough Years

ARSHILE GORKY

The Breakthrough Years

Organized by
MICHAEL AUPING

with essays by

DORE ASHTON
MICHAEL AUPING
MATTHEW SPENDER

Modern Art Museum of Fort Worth
Fort Worth, Texas

in association with

This exhibition has been co-organized by the Modern Art Museum of Fort Worth and the Albright-Knox Art Gallery, Buffalo, New York.

Editor: Karen Lee Spaulding, Albright-Knox Art Gallery
Designer: Alex Castro, CASTRO/ARTS, Baltimore

First published in the United States of America in 1995 by
Rizzoli International Publications, Inc.
300 Park Avenue South, New York, New York 10010

Library of Congress Cataloging-in-Publication Data
Ashton, Dore.
    Arshile Gorky : the breakthrough years / organized by Michael Auping : with texts by Dore Ashton, Michael Auping, Matthew Spender, p. cm.
    Catalogue of exhibition to be held at National Gallery of Art, Modern Art Museum of Fort Worth, and Albright-Knox Art Gallery, from May 1995 to March 1996.
    Includes bibliographical references and index.
    ISBN 0-8478-1875-6 (hardbound)
    ISBN 0-914782-92-4 (softbound)
    1. Gorky, Arshile, 1904–1948–Exhibitions. I. Gorky, Arshile, 1904–1948.
    II. Auping, Michael. III. Spender, Matthew. IV. Modern Art Museum of Fort Worth. V. Albright-Knox Art Gallery. VI. National Gallery of Art (U.S.)
    VII. Title. ND237.G613A4 1995
    759.13—dc20   94-22795 CIP

frontispiece:
Arshile Gorky, 1946
Photograph by Gjon Mili
Life Magazine © Time Warner

Printed in Italy

Contents

NATIONAL GALLERY OF ART
Washington, D.C.
May 7 – September 17, 1995

ALBRIGHT-KNOX ART GALLERY
Buffalo, New York
October 13 – December 31, 1995

MODERN ART MUSEUM OF FORT WORTH
Fort Worth, Texas
January 13 – March 17, 1996

This exhibition and publication were made possible,
in part, by a generous grant from the Luce Fund
for Scholarship in American Art, a program of the
Henry Luce Foundation, Inc.

LENDERS TO THE EXHIBITION

Mr. and Mrs. Michael J. Berberian
David Geffen, Los Angeles
Mr. and Mrs. Stanley R. Gumberg, Pittsburgh
Mr. and Mrs. Donald Jonas
Robert and Jane Meyerhoff, Phoenix, Maryland
Private Collection
Private Collection, courtesy Robert Miller Gallery
Private Collection, courtesy
        Allan Stone Gallery, New York
Private Collection, on loan to
        the National Gallery of Art, Washington
Denise and Andrew Saul

Albright-Knox Art Gallery, Buffalo, New York
Art Gallery of Ontario, Toronto
The Art Museum, Princeton University
The Baltimore Museum of Art
The Brooklyn Museum
Dallas Museum of Art
Solomon R. Guggenheim Museum, New York
Hirshhorn Museum and Sculpture Garden,
        Smithsonian Institution
Israel Museum Collection
The Menil Collection, Houston
The Metropolitan Museum of Art, New York
Munson-Williams-Proctor Institute, Museum of Art,
        Utica, New York
The Museum of Contemporary Art, Los Angeles
The Museum of Fine Arts, Houston
The Museum of Modern Art, New York
National Gallery of Art, Washington
The Nelson-Atkins Museum of Art,
        Kansas City, Missouri
Seattle Art Museum
Tate Gallery, London
Washington University Gallery of Art, St. Louis
Whitney Museum of American Art, New York
Yale University Art Gallery

Acquavella Galleries, Inc.
C & M Arts, New York
The John McEnroe Gallery, New York

Foreword

ABSTRACT EXPRESSIONISM is generally thought to be the highest point of American art. The powerful new forms and complex levels of content established by American artists working in the 1940s and 1950s continue to fascinate us a half century later, as we seek to understand more fully the sources and ultimate meanings of an imagery that has been boldly labeled "The Triumph of American Painting." Over the past two decades, scholars have researched the developments associated with this movement with a level of enthusiasm and scrutiny that has attended the study of Impressionism and Cubism, and art museums throughout the world are justifiably proud if they can devote some of their most prominent galleries to presenting the achievements of this period.

One of the most intriguing aspects of Abstract Expressionism is the question of its beginnings, and there is perhaps no more important an individual in this regard than Arshile Gorky, whose work of the 1940s is the subject of this exhibition. During his brief but potent career, Gorky assimilated the inventions of Cézanne, Picasso, Kandinsky, Miró, and the Surrealists. His synthesis of modern art's many inventive pathways, combined with his passionate embrace of nature, helped create a totally new vision for painting, one that would be shared by Willem de Kooning, Jackson Pollock, Clyfford Still, and Mark Rothko, among others.

The Modern Art Museum and the Albright-Knox Art Gallery are eminently suited to organize this exhibition. Both institutions have consistently sought to present the outstanding achievements of postwar American art through their exhibitions and publications, and both institutions have shown a special interest in Abstract Expressionism and related movements. We are proud to have the National Gallery of Art as a partner in this tour and extend a special thanks to our colleague, Earl A. Powell III. Following last year's retrospective of the work of Willem de Kooning, the National Gallery has placed *Arshile Gorky: The Breakthrough Years*, as it does all of its exhibitions, in very good company.

The exhibition has been conceived and organized by Michael Auping, Chief Curator of the Modern Art Museum of Fort Worth and former Chief Curator of the Albright-Knox Art Gallery, Buffalo. Mr. Auping has worked with dedication and enthusiasm over the past three years to realize this exhibition and the insightful catalogue that accompanies it. For over a decade, he has made Abstract Expressionism a special focus of his curatorial program and we are grateful to have his expertise for this project.

We are also indebted to the museums and private collectors that have so generously agreed to part with their works so that this exhibition could be possible. Works of such significance are rarely lent, and we are honored by their confidence in the importance of this presentation and accompanying catalogue. Finally, we extend our appreciation to the Luce Fund for Scholarship in American Art, a program of the Henry Luce Foundation, Inc., for their generous support of this project.

MARLA PRICE, Director
Modern Art Museum of Fort Worth

DOUGLAS G. SCHULTZ, Director
Albright-Knox Art Gallery

Preface and Acknowledgments

ONE OF A SMALL GROUP OF NEW YORK ARTISTS to pioneer a radically new development in American art, Arshile Gorky established a complex formal vocabulary that functioned as a critical umbilical cord between European Surrealism and the development of Abstract Expressionism. Alone among his fellow Abstract Expressionist painters — Pollock, de Kooning, Rothko, Still — Gorky achieved the pinnacle of his career in the 1940s, establishing him as a seminal figure in that movement. This exhibition focuses on the artist's coveted works from 1940 to 1947, what many think of as Gorky's breakthrough years. Remembered landscapes from his childhood home in Armenia fuse surrealist representation with abstract plumes of color, anticipating the enigmatic symbols and expressive gestures that would be a hallmark of Abstract Expressionism.

Critics and historians have always acknowledged the importance of Gorky's work of the 1940s, generally downplaying his earlier imagery of the late 1920s and 1930s. Nonetheless, Gorky exhibitions have tended to be large and comprehensive in nature. The largest and most important presentation was Diane Waldman's 1981 retrospective at the Guggenheim Museum, which included nearly 250 works. In 1989, the Fundacion Caja de Pensiones, Madrid, and the Whitechapel Art Gallery, London, shared a European retrospective of ninety-three works. Both projects presented substantial numbers of early works. By contrast, this exhibition is tightly focused. *Arshile Gorky: The Breakthrough Years* isolates a powerful moment not only in Gorky's brief life, but in the life of American art.

Along with representing a survey of the artist's most mature paintings, an additional focus of the exhibition will be on Gorky's drawings, as the period

1940–47 was an exceptionally rich period of drawing for the artist. Gorky's drawings play a key role in tracking the artist's process of imagemaking. What we hope to expose is the fascinating dialogue that Gorky creates between the two mediums. In some instances, the drawings are a means of recording details of nature in a telescopic fashion and then coaxing those images into a new hybrid form. Other drawings come after major paintings and are a way of further complicating a previous image on canvas.

To our museum colleagues and the astute private collectors who have parted with their masterpieces for the duration of this tour, I offer heartfelt gratitude on behalf of the audiences that will have an opportunity to see this concentration of many of Gorky's greatest works. One of the most spectacular paintings in the exhibition (in terms of both scale and imagery) is *The Liver is the Cock's Comb*, 1944, from the collection of the Albright-Knox Art Gallery. *The Liver* has not left Buffalo in over a decade and is a special addition to the exhibition. To the Director and Board of Directors of the Albright-Knox Art Gallery, I express my deep appreciation for allowing us to include this great work in all the presentations.

By nature, exhibitions are always a collaboration, but this one is especially gratifying. I could not have had more inspiring and exacting colleagues to contribute to this publication. Dore Ashton, whose writing time is in constant demand, has contributed what we have come to expect of her — a lucid, personal, and art historically grounded account of an artist who tends to resist classification. Matthew Spender, who is currently working on an extensive biography of the artist, has contributed his broad knowledge of Gorky's early years, allowing us to understand more fully the dramatic character of a life that has led to the artist's complex visionary imagery. Agnes Fielding and Maro Gorky both participated in this project with interest and generosity. Karekin Arzoomanian, chairman, Arshile Gorky Commemoration Committee, was particularly helpful in obtaining permissions to reprint the letters of Gorky, as translated by Karlen Mooradian. We are grateful for the cooperation in this regard of the Diocese of the Armenian Church of America (Eastern District), Archbishop Khajag Barsamian, Primate.

The staff of the Albright-Knox Art Gallery has continued to support my efforts in immeasurable ways. Editor of Publications Karen Lee Spaulding kept us moving with efficiency and good cheer. Among many other things, I will miss her willingness to indulge my capacity to ignore deadlines. The staff of the G. Robert Strauss, Jr., Memorial Library, most especially Librarian Kari Horowicz and Assistant Librarian Janice Lurie, performed impossible tasks of research and prepared the bibliography and exhibition history with their usual insight and special expertise. Editorial/Library Intern Talley Wettlaufer ably aided in the preparatory stages of the catalogue. Registrar Laura Catalano gave valuable and experienced advice about the transportation of such significant works of art. Curatorial Secretary Marge Hewlett tackled her first large project with ability and humor. To each of them, I extend my gratitude for all they have done.

At Universe Publishing, to Adele Ursone and James Stave, I offer my appreciation for their commitment to this important project and for their part in making it possible for this book to be published with Rizzoli International Publications. At Rizzoli, I am indebted to Katherine Adzima, Solveig Williams, and Elizabeth White. Alex Castro designed this publication — his fifth collaboration with the Albright-Knox — with his customary fine sensibility and keen understanding of his subject.

I would like to extend special thanks to Marla Price, Director of the Modern Art Museum of Fort Worth, and Douglas G. Schultz, Director of the Albright-Knox Art Gallery, for the spirit of cooperation they have demonstrated in sharing the responsibilities for this project. It is my good fortune to work for both of them.

At the National Gallery of Art, Mark Rosenthal has been pivotal in bringing this exhibition to Washington. Along with his colleagues at the NGA — Gaillard Ravenel, Marla Prather, and Ann Robertson — Mr. Rosenthal has seen to it that the exhibition's premiere in Washington will be a special event.

At the Modern Art Museum of Fort Worth, I have been exceptionally fortunate to inherit a highly efficient staff. I am particularly grateful to Susan Colegrove, Administrative Assistant, for helping me on virtually every aspect of the project. Andrea Karnes, Registrar, has had the difficult task of safely coordinating the shipments of the works. I thank the entire staffs of all three museums participating in this tour for the effort they have extended on behalf of this project.

MICHAEL AUPING, Chief Curator
Modern Art Museum of Fort Worth

Introduction

MICHAEL AUPING

SOME OF THE MOST SIGNIFICANT ART of the twentieth century has resulted from artists adapting to a new culture, while retaining powerful memories of their homeland. Picasso and Kandinsky in Paris; Beckmann in Amsterdam; Mondrian, Léger, and de Kooning in New York — a few prominent examples — all created masterworks that synthesized a past life with a new one. The life and art of Arshile Gorky constitute yet another remarkable example of the creative impulse that can result from dislocation. The Surrealist poet André Breton celebrated Gorky's imagery for its beguiling "hybrid" qualities. Without question, Gorky's paintings and drawings reflected the deep hybrid character of the artist himself. At their most poignant level, these images resulted from an intense need to connect memories of his ancient homeland of Armenia with his new American home and thus forge a separate but comprehensive identity between the two. For exiles and refugees, however, identities do not come easily. Indeed, there are only a few fairy-tale stories in this regard, and Gorky's is not one of them. In an era in which artists seemed to attract fame and tragedy in equal amounts, Gorky's story is particularly poignant.

Arshile Gorky was born Vosdanik Adoian in 1904 at Khorkom, Armenia. The third of four children and the only son of Lady Shushanik der Marderosian

Opposite: Detail, *One Year the Milkweed*, 1944. Oil on canvas, 37 × 47 inches. Collection National Gallery of Art, Washington. Ailsa Mellon Bruce Fund

and Sedrak Adoian, he was descended from a family of Armenian Apostolic Church priests on his mother's side and landed gentry on his father's. A potentially nurturing and protected childhood, however, was brutally interrupted by the Turkish invasions of Armenia. Fearing conscription into the Turkish army and being forced to fight against fellow Armenians, Gorky's father reluctantly left his wife and children to scout out a new life for his family in the United States. Gorky's close friend and biographer, Ethel Schwabacher, recorded that a "direct and traumatic effect of the father's departure" was the child's inability to speak until the age of five. [1] By the time he was fifteen years old, Gorky had witnessed the death of his thirty-nine-year-old mother by starvation, denying herself food to save her children during a forced march across Armenia.

It was his mother who established the identity of the household and who first kindled in Gorky the fantasy of being an artist. Gorky often referred to her profound influence: "Mother's thoughts were so correct, so valid for so many things in life and especially nature . . . She was the most aesthetically appreciative, the most poetically incisive master I have encountered in all my life . . . Mother was a poetess of aesthetics. Mother was queen of the aesthetic domain." [2] Gorky was his mother's son, and he would revere her appreciation of art, craft, and nature all his life. The Armenian landscape, too, left a particularly prominent impression on the young boy. From childhood, the land — and especially the gardens around his parents' house — represented a wellspring for the imagination. Regardless, the young Armenian would travel a great distance emotionally and geographically before his memories of Khorkom would help form the imagery that would later be known as "The Triumph of American Painting."

Gorky's challenges did not end when he arrived by boat in America in 1920 at the age of sixteen. Expelled from his "garden" and forced to be a nomad for a decade, he now struggled to find his way into the awesome possibilities of American culture. Gorky took to the challenge with admirable daring. Rather than seek "practical" employment, he would pursue the career of an artist. Offering an early model for the critic Harold Rosenberg's later dictum that "an artist is someone who invents an artist," the young Armenian, Vosdanik Adoian, took the name Arshile Gorky. In many ways, Gorky's chosen name served him practically and symbolically. Claiming to be the cousin of the radical Russian writer Maxim Gorky, gave the unknown an instant pedigree that attracted attention and perhaps opened a few doors. The new name also ironically foretold the classical and revolutionary character of his art, as well as the fragile life of an artist (Arschille, an Armenian variant of Achilles, refers to the powerful but flawed Homeric hero).

Sensing no irony or contradiction in his approach, Gorky assimilated modern art with surprisingly old-fashioned discipline. Essentially self-taught, he visited museums and studied reproductions, copying radical styles and techniques like a medieval apprentice. In the mid-1920s, he painted Impressionist pictures, then progressed to imitating Cézanne and Synthetic Cubism. Eventually, Picasso, Kandinsky, Miró, Matisse, and Léger became his artistic heroes before many of his American colleagues acknowledged their importance. Gorky's passionate and steep learning curve over the course of the 1920s and 1930s is punctuated by numerous portraits of himself, imaginary companions, and his family; the most poignant of these undoubtedly is *The Artist and His Mother*, ca. 1926–36. A haunting and melancholic tribute to her memory, this and other portrait works of the period — juxtaposed to the artist's disciplined studies of modern art — reflect an artist clearly adrift in a kind of purgatory between two lives.

As important as the 1930s were to Gorky's eventual maturity as an image maker, they also constituted a low point in his personal, financial, and artistic struggles. Gorky spoke about those years to Agnes, his second wife; she described them "as the bleakest, most spirit-crushing period of his life." [3] In the winter of 1938, Gorky wrote to his sister Vartoosh:

> . . . Nowadays an extremely melancholy mood has seized me and I can concentrate on nothing except my work. Dearest ones, lately I have been well and am working on excessively and am changing my painting style. Therefore, this constantly gives me extreme mental anguish. I am not satisfied and from now on I will never be satisfied a single day about my works. I desire to create deeper and purer work. [4]

Throughout the decade, however, Gorky never veered from a complete devotion to painting, often forgoing food for special brushes and paint. It was in the 1930s that he applied many layers to his canvases in an effort to locate a sensibility that reflected his increasingly complex psychological state; as well, these images would somehow come to embody and reflect the psychology of his time. Of course, it was not just Gorky who was anxious and searching. The war in Europe would allow New York to imagine itself as the new center of the art world. New York criticism and gossip were abuzz with how art there might radically overthrow that of the School of Paris. As an artist who understood modernism intuitively, as it were, Gorky was in a position to be a spearhead of new possibilities.

The last nine years of Gorky's life (ca. 1940–48) marked a powerfully expansive period for American art in general and for Gorky's art in particular. Geometric tendencies such as Cubism, Constructivism, and Neoplasticism, which had constituted an important source of inspiration for American artists during the 1930s, along with American Regionalist painting, were being supplanted by a more spontaneous, expressionist aesthetic. The New York art world began looking to the color-inspired gesture of Kandinsky, whose works could be seen at The Solomon R. Guggenheim Collection of Non-Objective Paintings, which opened on East Fifty-Fourth Street in 1939. At the same time, a new generation of European artists — identified as Surrealists — whose strange biomorphic and figurative imagery developed in the post-Freudian atmosphere of the 1930s, took center stage figuratively and literally in a New York that was becoming a home to exiled European radicals.

Surrealism, which had been launched officially in 1924 with the publication of André Breton's first *Surrealist Manifesto*, stressed spontaneity, accident, and coincidence in the belief that an ultimate reality could be achieved through the unification of two seemingly contradictory states — the dream and reality — into one state he referred to as "surreality." For Gorky, Surrealism pushed him — a talented but not yet convincingly original painter — to a new level of experimentation. Combining some of the psychologically charged ideas of Surrealism with his love of Miró and Kandinsky, Gorky opened the 1940s with an intriguingly hybrid image of description, memory, and pure abstraction, stretching Surrealism beyond its literary sources and leading American painting into one of the most experimental periods in its history.

For the decade between 1938 and 1948, Gorky's life and career can be likened to a shooting star, burning intensely bright but much too briefly. From about 1938 to 1942, Gorky focused on a series of paintings he titled "Garden in Sochi." It was initially through this group of works, and particularly the renditions after 1940, that the artist made the breakthrough to his most mature and imaginative images, in which remembered landscapes from his childhood in Armenia fuse surrealist fantasy with abstract bursts of line and color, anticipating the expressive gestures that are the hallmarks of the movement that would later be called Abstract Expressionism. Although titled after a Russian resort on the Black Sea, the "Garden in Sochi" series is an homage to his lost gardens.[5]

Although predominantly abstract, the "Sochi" paintings are replete with veiled references to the artist's Armenian experiences. For Gorky, Surrealism had become a means of allowing his elegantly spontaneous lines to recall various memory sequences. The "Sochi" paintings also include visual codes for pointed-toe Armenian slippers that his father wore as well as his mother's "soft Armenian butter churn, the pearl in the crown of our hard-working village women."[6] In a letter of 1942 to his sister Vartoosh, Gorky evokes the "Sochi" series and Khorkom in a poetic and deeply felt passage:

> Sweet Vartoosh, loving memories of our garden in Armenia's Khorkom haunt me frequently. Recall Father's garden down the path from our house and the Tree of the Cross upon which the authentic Armenian villagers attached the colorful pennants of their clothing. Within our garden could be found the glorious and living panoply of Armenian nature, so unknown to all yet so in need of being known. Beloved sister, in my art I often draw our garden and recreate its precious greenery and life. Can a son forget the soil which sires him?

> Beloveds, the stuff of thought is the seed of the artist. Dreams form the bristles of the artist's brush. And as the eye functions as the brain's sentry, I communicate my most private perceptions through art, my view of the world. In trying to probe beyond the ordinary and the known, I create an inner infinity. I probe within the confines of the finite to create an infinity. Liver. Bones. Living rocks and living plants and animals. Living dreams. Vartoosh dearest, to this I owe my debt to our Armenian art. Its hybrids, its many opposites. The inventions of our folk imagination. These I attempt to capture directly, I mean the folklore and physical beauty of our homeland, in my works.[7]

After 1940, Gorky's life and his art experienced a profound sense of renewal. In 1941, he fell in love with Agnes Magruder. Beautiful and considerably younger than Gorky, Agnes gave her husband a new sense of mission, and the possibility of a new family may have brought his memories of Khorkom even closer to the surface. The fact that his personal life was entering a new stage coincided with a rapid acceleration of changes and new inventions in his art. These changes may have been partially precipitated by a survey exhibition of his work held at the San Francisco Museum of Art in August of 1941. Although the exhibition met with generally favorable reviews, Gorky undoubtedly viewed the presentation with his often incisively critical eye. Flattered by the opportunity to show his work, Gorky, like most artists in that situation, longed for what was not there — the next invention. According to the sculptor Raoul Hague, Gorky "wanted to show how far an image could be stretched . . . . He realized in San Francisco he had not stretched it far enough." [8]

Following their marriage in 1941, Gorky and Agnes began a series of retreats from the city; initially at the home of Saul Schary in Connecticut, and later at Agnes's parents' home, Crooked Run Farm in Virginia. During these visits, Gorky completed many drawings and a number of paintings. Thinking about his homeland and his renewed creativity, Gorky wrote "it is as if some ancient Armenian spirit within me moves my hand to create so far from our homeland the shapes of nature we loved in the gardens, wheatfields, and orchards of our Adoian family in Khorkom. Our beautiful Armenia which we lost and which I will repossess in my art." [9] Nature, and its ability to catalyze his memories of Armenia, became the central element in inspiring Gorky's breakthrough years of the 1940s.

Around this same time, Gorky also met the Chilean Surrealist artist Matta Echaurren. Painting and drawing from nature brought a new sense of inspiration and subject matter to Gorky's art, while Matta sparked a technical change in Gorky's paintings. Matta, who had great appreciation for the spontaneity of Gorky's drawings, suggested that Gorky try to liberate his painting style by mixing turpentine with his paints to achieve a more fluid and explosive gesture. [10] Taking Matta's suggestion, Gorky completed a number of paintings from nature in which fluid, spontaneous veils of thin paint operate between keen observation and expressionist fantasy.

Gorky's paintings of the early 1940s also reflect his fascination with Kandinsky's early paintings and watercolors, in which explosive colors and lines denote an emotional response to nature rather than direct observation. Kandinsky's *The Waterfall* of 1909 may have partially inspired Gorky's great

Waterfall of 1942–43.[11] *Waterfall* constitutes one of Gorky's most brilliant accomplishments in combining emotional spontaneity and direct observation. As Diane Waldman described, "We can sense the path of the water as it cascades down the fall, flows in and around the rocks and comes to rest in the eddies and pools at its base."[12] We *can* truly sense the cascading, yet it is not described by Gorky in any detail. Indeed, *Waterfall* is an inspired abstraction in rich greens and blues.

Gorky's imagery was also transformed through the drawings he completed during the restorative time he spent in the Virginia landscape. "The Ingres of the unconscious,"[13] was how Gorky's biographer, Ethel Schwabacher, characterized him: an appropriate description for an artist who saw drawing as the scaffolding for all his imagery. While Gorky became known as an astute colorist, his drawings show that color is always enhanced by graphic means. He once wrote "Drawing is the basis of art. A bad painter cannot draw. But a good drawer can always paint."[14] During the 1930s, Gorky's precise line — much like that of Ingres — was put to the service of intimate and elegantly outlined portraits of himself, his friends, and his family. By the early 1940s, that linearity had retained its descriptive clarity but was now being applied to a detailed investigation of ambiguous plant and insect forms. Gorky's experiences at Crooked Run Farm inspired him to "look into the grass,"[15] as he put it, and magnify nature in all its organic and erotic detail. His drawings of this time are marked by his signature precision and delicate outlining, created by an exceptionally sharp pencil point and aided by subtle shading and hatching.

As Gorky's cataloguer Jim Jordan wrote, "In the work at Crooked Run Farm, Gorky found the language of detail, the organization of space, and coloristic power of his triumphant mature style."[16] Throughout the 1940s, Gorky spent increasing amounts of time working from the landscape, using it as a matrix of stimulation. Nature allowed the artist to reconcile the different worlds his imag-

At Crooked Run Farm, Hamilton, Virginia, ca. 1943–44. Photograph courtesy Maro Gorky Spender and Matthew Spender

ination inhabited: his memories of Armenia, the psychological fantasies of Surrealism, as well as his formalist needs to experiment with line and color. Gorky stayed at Crooked Run Farm for nine months in 1944, a year in which he produced some of his greatest works.

While many of Gorky's drawings were done on site, his paintings were most often created in the solitude of his studio. Here, memory seemed increasingly to trigger images from his psyche; these were then translated into rich gestural fields of color. While *Waterfall*, 1942–43, evoked nature as Gorky may have encountered it (using Kandinsky as a springboard), works such as *How My Mother's Embroidered Apron Unfolds in My Life*, 1944, results from a powerful sense of reverie. Gorky described the work as a deep memory image:

> I tell stories to myself, often, while I paint, often nothing to do with the painting. Have you ever listened to a child telling that this is a house and this is a man and this is a cow in the sunlight . . . while his crayon wanders in an apparently meaningless scrawl all over the paper? My stories are often from my childhood. My mother told me many stories while I pressed my face into her long apron with my eyes closed. She had a long white apron like the one in her portrait, and another embroidered one. Her stories and the embroidery on her apron got confused in my mind with my eyes closed. All my life her stories and her embroidery keep unraveling pictures in my memory. If I sit before a blank white canvas . . . .[17]

In the winter of 1944, Gorky met André Breton, the poet and self-appointed spokesperson of Surrealism. Although Gorky was well acquainted with Surrealist theory and practice by that time, he established a special relationship with Breton. Over the next months, Breton convinced gallery owner Julien Levy — who handled works by many of the Surrealists — to represent Gorky's work. In the spring of 1945, Levy presented what was arguably the most important exhibition of Gorky's work in his lifetime. The exhibition included such masterworks as *How My Mother's Embroidered Apron Unfolds in My Life*, 1944; *Love of the New Gun*, 1944; *One Year the Milkweed*, 1944; *The Sun, The Dervish in the Tree*, 1944, and *Water of the Flowery Mill*, 1944, among others.

This 1945 exhibition and the startlingly original works included in it established Gorky's pioneering presence within the developing movement of Abstract Expressionism that would also include Willem de Kooning, Jackson

Pollock, Mark Rothko, Clyfford Still, and Barnett Newman, among others. Breton wrote what still stands as one of the most insightful introductions to Gorky's work. He coined the term "hybrids" to describe the sensually ambiguous character of Gorky's imagery:

> Most artists are still for turning around the hands of the clock, in every sense of the phrase, without having the slightest concern for the spring hidden in the opaque case. The eye-spring. . . Arshile Gorky for me the first painter to whom the secret has been completely revealed! Truly the eye was not made to take inventory like an auctioneer, nor to flirt with delusions and false recognitions like a maniac. It was made to cast a lineament, a conducting wire between the most heterogeneous things. . .
>
> Easy-going amateurs will come here for their meager rewards: in spite of all warning to the contrary they will insist on seeing in these compositions a still-life, a landscape, or a figure instead of daring to face the *hybrid* forms in which all human emotion is precipitated. By "hybrids" I mean the resultants provoked in an observer contemplating a natural spectacle with extreme concentration, the resultants being a combination of the spectacle and a flux of childhood and other memories, and the observer being gifted to a rare degree with the grace of emotion.[18]

Breton's words could have been used to describe the work of de Kooning, Pollock, or Still of the later 1940s and early 1950s. Of all the artists who would later be labeled Abstract Expressionists, it was Gorky who first lit the path through what Breton called "the analogical world." Breton specifically discussed what has, over the years, been considered Gorky's signature painting, *The Liver is the Cock's Comb*, 1944. A monumental field of plant and human body parts punctuated by explosive flames of color, *The Liver* represents a grand summation of the artist's meditations on nature, human emotion, and the erotic side of Surrealism.

On July 4, 1945, Gorky wrote to his sister Vartoosh, "This is the first year that I am working without any financial worries . . . Mr. Levy sold seven of my pictures."[19] Inspired by his brief success, Gorky continued over the next three years to push toward new formal inventions, always maintaining strong threads of autobiography and fantasy. While some works became more painterly, often involving exceedingly subtle color transitions, others relied for their emotional impact on a delicate calligraphy. *The Plow and the Song*, 1947, combines both these qualities, while continuing to explore the artist's meditations on his homeland. Here, the remembered shape of an Armenian plow is transformed into a lyrical line tracing its way through delicately colored abstract passages. Following the artist's interest in the erotics of landscape in *The Liver is the Cock's Comb*, *The Plow and the Song* alludes to an image of fertility and development. The image had been haunting Gorky as early as 1944, as a letter to his sister of that year indicates:

> Vartoosh dear, I have been occupied in drawing the Armenian plows which we used in our Adoian fields near our house. Recall? I have carved one from wood which I will send to Karlen. You cannot imagine the fertility of forms that leap from our Armenian plows, the plows our ancestors used for thousands of years of toil and gaiety and hardship and poetry. A plow must be the fitting tombstone for the Armenian man from Khorkom.[20]

The titles of a number of the artist's later works — *Charred Beloved*, 1946; *The Unattainable*, 1946; *Delicate Game*, 1946; *The Limit*, 1947; *Agony*, 1947 — reflect Gorky's increasingly introspective and, at times, melancholic moods, as well as the series of tragic events that would befall him in his later years. In January 1945, a fire in his studio destroyed hundreds of his drawings, sketches, and books. In February of the same year, he underwent an operation for cancer. In the wake of these devastations, Gorky nonetheless produced many important drawings and some of his best paintings. Gorky and his family returned to Crooked Run Farm that summer where the artist produced 242 drawings. He continued to expand on his vocabulary of hybrid forms, grafting plant, animal, and human anatomy into puzzlingly sensual constructs.

In February of 1948, Gorky had the last one-person show of his lifetime at the Julien Levy Gallery. Including such masterworks as *The Liver is the Cock's Comb*, 1944; *Garden in Sochi*, 1941, and *Delicate Game*, 1946, the show was a select survey of Gorky's career. The preeminent critic and spokesperson of Abstract Expressionism, Clement Greenberg, reviewed the show in *The Nation*: "What is new about these paintings is the unproblematic voluptuousness with which they celebrate and display the process of painting for their own sake. With this sensuous richness . . . Gorky at last . . .takes his place . . . among the very few contemporary American painters whose work is of more than national importance."[21]

Unfortunately, Gorky's tragedies were not over. In June that year, he and Levy were in an automobile accident. Gorky's neck was broken and his painting arm was paralyzed. Approximately three weeks later, he and Agnes separated, with the children leaving with her. The disintegration of his marriage and the immobilizing accident proved too much for Gorky to overcome. On July 21, 1948, he committed suicide in his Sherman, Connecticut, studio at the age of forty-four. He wrote in white chalk on a painting crate, *Goodbye My Beloveds.*

His friend and fellow painter Willem de Kooning insisted that Gorky was beyond categorizing in terms of movements. "He had all those things before the Surrealists and the Surrealists told him he had it already. I mean he had a fantastic instinct, a gift of seeing it the right way."[22] Unfortunately, categories die hard in art history, and conventional wisdom has always situated Gorky in a kind of no-man's land between Surrealism of the 1930s and Abstract Expressionism of the 1950s. It is undoubtedly true that his peculiarly hybrid imagery provided an important stylistic and philosophical umbilical cord between the two movements. So the term transitional is at least partly accurate, but it is also a term of last resort. Gorky was never a joiner and his art, more so than most, has always resisted classification. In a letter to *Art News* following Gorky's death, de Kooning scolded an art press that didn't seem to understand the importance of what came out of Gorky's studio at 36 Union Square in New York.

In a piece on Arshile Gorky's memorial show — and it was a very little piece indeed — it was mentioned that I was one of his influences. Now that is plain silly. When, about fifteen years ago, I walked into Arshile's studio for the first time, the atmosphere was so beautiful that I got a little dizzy and when I came to, I was bright enough to take the hint immediately. If the bookkeepers think it necessary continuously to make sure of where things and people come from, well then, I come from 36 Union Square. It is incredible to me that other people live there now. I am glad that it is about impossible to get away from his powerful influence. As long as I keep it with myself I'll be doing all right. Sweet Arshile, bless your dear heart.[23]

If Gorky had inspired only de Kooning, we would be considerably in his debt. He ultimately inspired many more, laying the aesthetic groundwork for the greatest revolution in American painting. Although he was gone before the term Abstract Expressionism was coined, and before the now famous *Life* photograph of "The Irascibles" was published, he left an eloquent legacy of images to that movement.

Gorky died before this picture of "The Irascibles" — all key figures in the Abstract Expressionist movement — was taken in 1950. *Left to right: top row:* de Kooning, Gottlieb, Reinhardt, Sterne; *middle row:* Pousette-Dart, Baziotes, Pollock, Still, Motherwell, Tomlin; *bottom row:* Stamos, Jimmy Ernst, Newman, Brooks, Rothko. Photograph by Nina Leen, *Life* Magazine © Time Warner

1. Ethel K. Schwabacher, *Arshile Gorky* (New York: The Macmillan Company for the Whitney Museum of American Art, 1957), p. 25.

2. Letter to Vartoosh Mooradian, November 2, 1946, in Karlen Mooradian, *The Many Worlds of Arshile Gorky* (Chicago: Gilgamesh Press Limited, 1980), pp. 309–10.

3. Letter from Agnes Gorky Phillips to Patricia Passlof in *The 30's: Painting in New York* (New York: Poindexter Gallery, 1957), n.p. Also quoted in Diane Waldman, "Arshile Gorky: Poet in Paint" in *Arshile Gorky* (New York: The Solomon R. Guggenheim Museum and Harry N. Abrams, Inc., 1981), p. 41.

4. Letter (to Vartoosh, Manuk, and Karlen Mooradian), February 28, 1938, in Karlen Mooradian, *Arshile Gorky Adoian* (Chicago: Gilgamesh Press Limited, 1978), p. 255.

5. Gorky titled the series "Garden in Sochi" rather than "Garden in Khorkom" because he felt an American audience would be more attentive and respectful of a Russian home than an Armenian one. See his letter to Vartoosh Mooradian, July 1943, in Karlen Mooradian, "A Special Issue on Arshile Gorky," in *Ararat* (New York), Fall 1971, p. 29.

6. Ibid.

7. Letter to Vartoosh Mooradian, February 9, 1942, in *Ararat*, p. 28.

8. Raoul Hague, in conversation with the author, March 1987.

9. Letter to Vartoosh Mooradian, April 22, 1944, in *Ararat*, p. 32.

10. Julien Levy, *Arshile Gorky* (New York: Harry N. Abrams, Inc., 1966), p. 24.

11. Gail Levin, "Kandinsky and Abstract Expressionism" in *Theme and Improvisation: Kandinsky & the American Avant-Garde 1912 - 1950* (Boston: Bulfinch Press for the Dayton Art Institute, 1992), p. 209.

12. Waldman, "Arshile Gorky: Poet in Paint," p. 52.

13. Quoted in John Elderfield, *The Modern Drawing: 100 Works on Paper from The Museum of Modern Art* (New York: The Museum of Modern Art, 1983), p. 184.

14. Letter to Vartoosh Mooradian, February 9, 1942, in *Ararat*, p. 28.

15. James Johnson Sweeney, "Five American Painters," *Harper's Bazaar* (New York), April 1944, pp. 122, 124.

16. Jim M. Jordan, "Arshile Gorky at Crooked Run Farm," *Arts Magazine* (New York), March 1976, p. 203.

17. Levy, *Arshile Gorky*, p. 34.

18. André Breton, "The Eye-Spring: Arshile Gorky" in *Arshile Gorky* (New York: Julien Levy Gallery, March 1945), n.p.

19. Quoted in Lisa Dennison Tabak, "Chronology" in Waldman, *Arshile Gorky*, p. 265.

20. Letter to Vartoosh Mooradian, December 1944, in *Ararat*, p. 32.

21. Clement Greenberg, "Art," *The Nation* (New York), March 20, 1948, p. 31.

22. Excerpts from interview by Karlen Mooradian with Willem de Kooning, July 19, 1966, in *Ararat*, Fall 1971, p. 49.

23. Letter to the editor, *Art News* (New York), April 1944, pp. 122, 124.

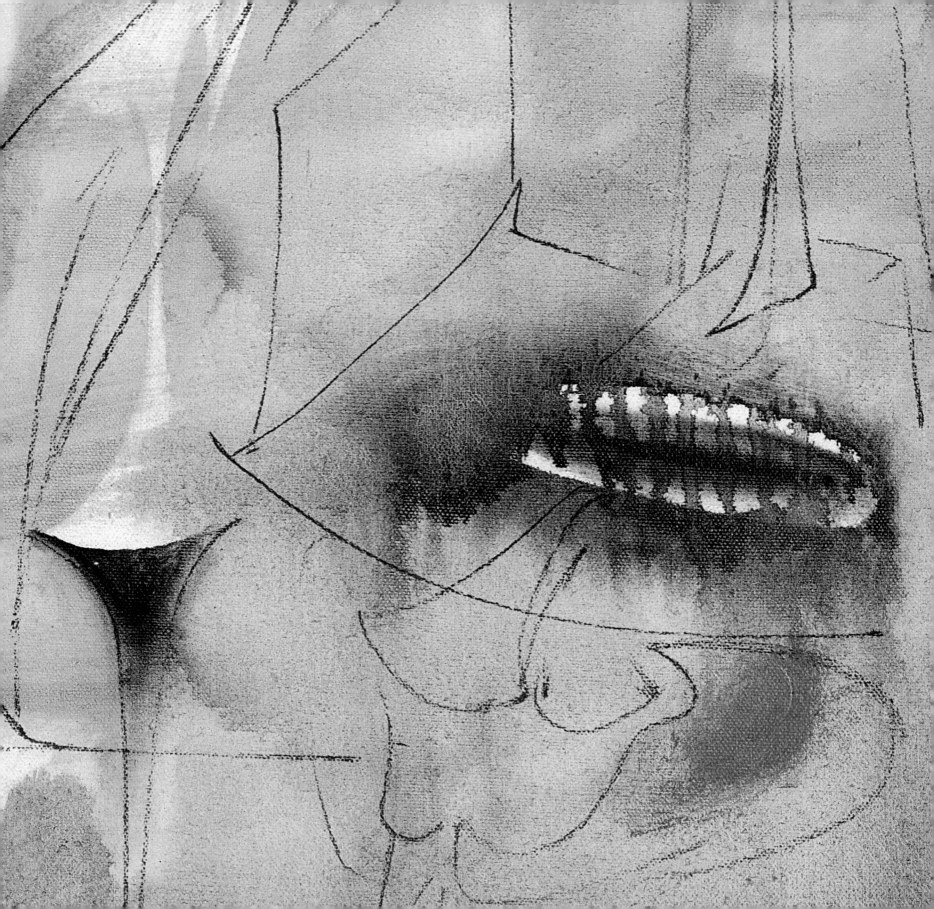

Arshile Gorky's Early Life

MATTHEW SPENDER

ALTHOUGH ARSHILE GORKY OFTEN TALKED about his childhood, he hated to be pinned down as to dates and places. The language he used was the language of myth. His father was a tall man on a white horse who rode away into the mists one day, never to return. His mother had bright blue eyes and Circassian blood in her veins. His uncle owned a factory in Georgia where, as a young man, Stalin used to work. During the revolution he saw the Red army fight the White in the streets of the village where he was born. His name was Gorky, and he received letters from his uncle Maxim, postmarked Venice. He himself was Georgian — as Russian — was anything but Armenian, at a time when, in the New World, the only adjective attached to the noun "Armenian" was the painful word "starving."

Gorky was not the only one to disguise the past. His three sisters each held tenaciously to their own private myths. In the case of Vartoosh, the sister who later lived in Chicago, her traumatic memories resulted in an over-idealization of Shushanik Marderosian, their mother. This vision was inherited by her son Karlen Mooradian, whose many versions of his uncle's life are corroded by fantasy, rage, and a deep need to retrieve a lost world.

Almost every fact about Gorky's life needs to be qualified. He was born Vostanig Adoian — but no one ever knew him as Vostanig, only as Manoog. His

Opposite: Detail, *Making the Calendar*, 1947. Oil on canvas, 34 × 41 inches. Collection Munson-Williams-Proctor Institute, Museum of Art, Utica, New York. Edward W. Root Bequest

birthday was April, except that sometimes it was in October. The year of birth declared on his naturalization certificate is 1904, but Gorky always looked older than his supposed age. In the part of Armenia where he came from, birthdays were not celebrated. Accuracy in these matters depended on working things out later, in America, where dates are needed on documents. In the back of the classroom at the village school in Khorkom, he had seemed much larger than the other boys. He sat there quietly whittling a stick and was not interested in learning.

Gorky's childhood took place between two terrible massacres, that of 1895–96, and that of 1915–16. If ever a psychopathological analysis of Gorky is written, it will have to discuss the fact that he was doubly a victim, in that his mother had already suffered atrociously in the first of these massacres. He inherited from her a sense of guilt and obligation, long before the second massacre sealed, with her death, a complex knot of repression and ambition, of hope, regret, and despair.

From the middle of the nineteenth century, the Ottoman government became preoccupied by the presence of a large Christian minority in the central and eastern provinces of Turkey. In some areas, especially around Van, this appeared to amount to more than half the population, the remainder composed of Kurdish nomadic tribes. Less than five percent of the population was Turkish. In this situation, a policy of persecution of the Armenians was initiated, using the Kurds as a spearhead, and encouraging them to expropriate and occupy Armenian lands wherever possible. The Armenians were excessively taxed, and — being Christian — in the case of injustice, they had no redress in a Muslim court of law. Traditionally, these taxes had been levied by the Kurdish tribes among whom the Armenians lived, but towards the end of the century the Turkish offi-

Map of Gorky's province of Van, Armenia, drawn by Karlen Mooradian. In Karlen Mooradian, *Arshile Gorky Adoian* (Chicago: Gilgamesh Press, 1978), p. 120. Reprinted with permission from the Diocese of the Armenian Church of America (Eastern District), Archbishop Khajag Barsamian, Primate.

cials tried to levy the taxes directly. This loss of privilege was resisted by the Kurds, and often an unfortunate area was obliged to pay taxes twice over.

In 1895, a first resistance by the Armenians of the Sassoun and Moush areas of Lake Van, easily anticipated, was as easily suppressed, with much loss of life. After this "event," large areas of land west and north of the lake were emptied of their Armenian inhabitants.

Gorky's mother Shushanik was married at the age of fourteen to a mountaineer from the Shattack area south of the lake. Like Moush and Sassoun, Shattack was considered to be an area of potential resistance to the central government and was therefore singled out for particular attention in 1895–96. Shushanik saw her husband killed in front of her eyes, together with all the other men in his family.

Left a widow with two children at the age of sixteen, she was quickly married off to Sedrak Adoian, a farmer and trader from Khorkom, a village situated between the lake and the main road from Van to Bitlis. Khorkom was not considered a particular center of Armenian resistance and was not devastated as Shattack had been.

Even so, many of Gorky's relatives on his father's side were killed. An uncle who had returned from Istanbul, where he had been working in a small import-export firm, was found dead, with no wound on him, under a pile of other bodies of the villagers.

Gorky was born six or seven years after the massacres, the memory of which was muted. No Turks lived in Khorkom. There were no Kurds there either, although Shushanik's town Vostan nearby was in the process of becoming forcibly Kurdish. In spite of all this tension, if left to themselves, the Kurds and Armenians often came to some kind of an arrangement. The Kurds were herdsmen; the Armenians tilled the land. Some cooperation was possible. Gorky's uncles spoke excellent Kurdish and had Kurds as friends. Although the archives give a gloomy picture, the survivors I have spoken to from the Van area hold mysteriously little rancor against the Kurds, even though the murderers of Armenians were so often Kurds.

Gorky's father left for the United States in 1908, after the first revolution of the Young Turk party. In this early phase, Turks and Armenians were aligned. Many Armenians took advantage of the relaxation of controls on emigration to travel to the United States, not with the intention of remaining there forever, but to earn money to bring back to burgeoning families. Gradually, the Adoian household in Khorkom emptied of its menfolk, including Gorky's uncle Grikor, whose supposed mistreatment of Shushanik is described by Karlen Mooradian and Hakob, Sedrak's son by an earlier marriage. The Adoian house must have contained nothing but women, and care of the land would have been a problem. In the fall of 1910, Shushanik moved away from Khorkom to live in the Armenian quarter of Van, where the schools were more reliable and there were more prospects for the future of her children.

Throughout his life, Gorky clung lovingly to his memories of Khorkom. Every garden, every spring, the sand on the shore, the color of the lake, the stones, the orchid growing in the shape of an anchor against a rock, the whispering poplars, the dead pine-needle tree with vertical branches clothed in fragments of torn rags, were images to which he constantly returned. This is surprising if one considers that he left Khorkom when he was only six years old. Khorkom, for Gorky, even at that tender age, was a source of nostalgic reverie. To return there on a donkey for the long summers was the dream of numerous students from the villages who had been sent to study in Van at the American Mission school.

It would be wonderful to be able to state that Gorky's studies at the American Mission school were "formative years." As far as I can tell, however, he enjoyed the carpentry department, where his uncle Aharon taught, more than he enjoyed the other classes. The missionaries were aware that their Armenian pupils needed training in order to find work later in this remote and backward province. Thus, weaving and carpentry shops flourished. The students were trained to become good craftsmen, which Gorky certainly was, and good Protestants, which interested him not at all. The school had only just attained college status when, in 1915, this fragile world came to an end.

The Turks, to this day, refer to the elimination of the Armenian minority as a "relocation" program. This is not the place to contest such a view. During the "relocation" of the Van district, Khorkom was sacked. Most of Gorky's family were lost: seven cousins on his mother's side were killed in Vostan, and the family church there destroyed; Uncle Grikor, who had just returned from the United States in time to be killed; Aunt Yeghus, who had been left in charge of the house in Khorkom, together with her daughter and two grandchildren; and

"Rus" Adoian, the cousin who had been left in charge of the land, whose five children would die of cholera at Etchmiazin a few weeks later.

Gorky himself, with his sisters and his mother, survived because they were living in Van city, which resisted a five-week siege until a Russian army relieved them. During a lull in the campaign, Shushanik walked with her little family to Yerevan, two hundred miles to the north. There, however, she fell into a strange state of apathy, perhaps deriving from shock. Her family church back in Vostan, now destroyed, had meant much to her. She was lost without her background. The double destruction of 1895 and 1915 must have placed an intolerable weight on her resistance. While she declined, the responsibility of supporting the family fell to Gorky, with the occasional help of his maternal uncle Aharon, who worked for the Near East Relief Fund. Shushanik died in 1919, of starvation and grief. Soon after, the remaining children set sail for America.

Gorky, ca. 1930s.
Photograph courtesy
Maro Gorky Spender and
Matthew Spender

Once in the United States, Gorky lived with the rest of his family in Watertown, Massachusetts. Nearby at Cranston, Rhode Island, lived his father Sedrak, with Hakob, Gorky's elder half brother, on a small farm not far from the iron foundry where they both worked. Gorky's father, by now an elderly man, was a grinder, while Hakob cast wheels for use in the textile industry. Gorky's elder half sister Akho kept a boarding house for Armenian bachelors in Watertown, and Gorky lived now here, now there. None of the family spoke good English. Hakob, in later years, would ask his son to read the newspaper to him, and when Akho needed to pass a test to attain American citizenship, she had to learn all the answers by heart. The Armenians of Watertown lived in a circumscribed world, which became still further locked within itself during the Depression. Like many others, the Adoians worked hard at unrewarding jobs, and after working hours, they recreated a lost paradise on their small farm, talking among themselves about a distant land.

With extraordinary force of will, this bright but not well-educated young man now suddenly became a painter. Why? There was nothing in his background to suggest this was a normal, let alone an unusual but admirable step to take. On the contrary, nobody in his family could ever bring themselves to think of what he did as "work," then, or even today.

The decision, I feel sure, was made many years before Gorky came to the United States — although whether he could have followed this path had he remained in Armenia, saddled with responsibility, is doubtful. One can only speculate on fragmentary facts. Gorky was late in learning how to speak. His talent was, in many ways, non-verbal, or perhaps pre-verbal, in that he drew before he first spoke. His mother had not been happy in her second marriage and may have regretted the loss of her first husband, and of her father, and of her family church. Gorky sometimes said that his mother referred to his soul as "black," when he showed reluctance to follow the ambitious path she had laid out for him, which was to study, rather than to make things with his hands. Soon after he learned to speak, his father left the house, never to return. So there is, in Gorky's life, the suggestion of the absent father, the overachieving mother, and a child who preferred to carve or to draw, rather than to speak. And, in the distant background, a genocide.

Gorky with his sister, Vartoosh Adoian Mooradian (left) and Sirun Mussikian (right) in Watertown, Massachusetts, 1930. Photograph courtesy Maro Gorky Spender and Matthew Spender

For the moment, he earned money at the Hood Rubber Company, a large firm in Watertown where many Armenian immigrants worked. His elder sister Satenik remained there for forty-five years. As for Gorky, they "let him go," as the metaphor of the time put it, after he had failed to come back from a coffee break and was found drawing on the large black tiles of the roof.

I doubt if the two or three years of intermittent study in schools near Boston were of great help to Gorky. He never went to Brown University, as he sometimes claimed. Gorky the artist was self-taught, just as "Gorky" the man was a self-created identity, superimposed on one he never revealed. Why he chose the name "Gorky" is mysterious. One family myth has it that his first choice of a name was "Archie Gunn," after the hero of a cowboy movie. This suggests that *any* name would have suited him, so long as it was not Armenian. But it is also true that he admired Maxim Gorky, whom he may have read while at school in Yerevan. As far as I can tell, the choice of the name precedes his friendship with John Graham, David Burliuk, and the "Russian circle" with whom he was connected in the late 1920s, otherwise it would be plausible to suggest that "Gorky" was their idea.

To change his name meant, I am sure, that Gorky consciously stepped back from his Armenian heritage. Many took offense. Uncle Aharon often reproached him for it. The writer William Saroyan, who knew and disliked Gorky, felt that to deny the past was wrong, at a time when Gorky's growing reputation could have helped all Armenians in America to state their identity with pride. Back in Watertown, only Akabi took his side, occasionally even sending him paints, after he had moved to New York. Otherwise, when he returned to Watertown and strode along Dexter Avenue in a long, romantic cloak, he was a figure of ridicule. To the Armenian community that had remained, he looked like nothing so much as Jesus Christ.

In New York, he obtained a job from Edmund Graecen, an excellent impressionist painter who had started an art school in Grand Central Station. His entrance in Graecen's life was traditional: cap in hand, he asked for a job — with presumably some of the excellent copies from old masters that he had made in Watertown under his arm. Frans Hals, El Greco perhaps, or maybe van Dyck — most of them were burned accidentally later. He taught at Grand Central from 1926 to 1932 and returned there at the beginning of the war to teach camouflage.

In 1926, he was interviewed for the first and, very nearly, the last time. As Maxim Gorky's nephew, he was worth an article in a newspaper. He talked about Cézanne, spoke affectionately about his uncle, and reprimanded the American public for buying painters who were dead, instead of heroes who were still alive. The journalist shrewdly observed that the paintings around the studio were less outspoken than the artist who had painted them, but then Gorky in life always assumed a forward position. In correcting his drawing class at Grand Central, he would march in twice a day, instantly say what was wrong in a student's drawing and perhaps correct the composition himself with a few masterly strokes, which would be rare for a teacher to do today. He would tell his pupils that few were ever likely to become painters, and that he himself was "out at sea in a rowboat, far from shore." And then march out again.

He made few converts, but those who listened to him were touched for life. Among these were Hans Burkhardt, who talked to me about Gorky only a week or two before he died in 1994, and Willem de Kooning, who (so I am told) passes and repasses in his mind many small incidents of their association. The lives of all three men possess elements in common: in each case, a remote father, a formidable but victimized mother and, at the end of adolescence, definitive exile from Europe to the United States. Enough, one would have thought, to make a strong bond among equals. But Gorky was unwilling or unable to place the idea of equality at the core of any relationship. He was the leader, and the others followed. Once, walking along behind Gorky in the street, de Kooning was nearly run down by a taxi. He was convinced that Gorky had stepped into the path of an oncoming cab on purpose, in order to emphasize the distance that lay between them.

The two strongest friendships of the early 1930s were with Stuart Davis and John Graham. Gorky wrote an article defending Davis and left a portfolio of Graham's drawings with a dealer to whom perhaps he was too shy to show his own work. In 1928, Graham announced publicly that the three of them were about to create a new modern movement in American art. Gorky absorbed much from Graham. I suspect that it was Graham who introduced him to Giorgio de Chirico and Paolo Uccello, two painters whose reputations would have been remote in 1930. But, unfortunately, all this interchange can only be guessed at. In the early 1940s, there was a falling out between them, followed by silence. In the writings of John Graham in the Archives of American Art, Gorky's name is hugely missing, although there are curious echoes of arguments which Gorky used from time to time: that Shakespeare was a terrible author who did not respect the "composition" of the stage, or that Dickens stole everything from Russian writers such as Dostoevsky. Gorky used similar verbal outrage in order to keep intellectuals at bay. These people, like so many others, were among those whom he wished to keep at a distance.

Gorky broke with Stuart Davis earlier. Davis had become increasingly involved in political activity during the 1930s, and he thought Gorky's detachment from committee work was somehow "frivolous." In this, he was surely wrong. Having suffered so much from politics in his childhood, Gorky can be forgiven for remaining detached from left-wing activities in New York, so rich in theory, so confused in action. Still, he might have refrained from saying that this produced only "poor art for poor people," a remark guaranteed to wreck any friendship.

During the 1930s, Gorky's two strongest relationships with women were with the painter Michael West and with his first wife, Marney George. The subordinate roles he eventually assigned to both of them proved for these independent

American women too onerous to bear. In both cases, a romantic courtship was followed by a reversion to the patriarchal expectations of his upbringing: an idea of family structure still typical of the eastern Mediterranean, even today, where the man of the family is the hero and the boss, the woman his devoted companion. Michael West walked out. Gorky threw Marney George out himself, having hastily packed all her possessions with his own hands, thrusting them into the hall after her. Both, in later years, felt that something had been missed, or left unsaid or unclarified, in this abrupt end to what might have been.

All this time, he was learning. The traditional view of Gorky's career was that these were years of "apprenticeship," in which he brilliantly absorbed all the styles of the painters he most admired. This is a view he fostered himself, with pithy phrases such as "if Picasso drips" his paint, "then I drip." But what makes the early work so interesting is that they, like the later work so admired by André Breton, are "hybrids." The masters are made to fight against one another. The concrete volumes of Picasso are combined with the empty spaces of Miró. The flat areas of form in Gorky's Newark Airport murals are much looser and wilder than the tight example of Fernand Léger, which Gorky was so clearly following.

Gorky felt that clarity and precision of shapes were essential. He talked with Graham and Davis about the "edge" of paint, the precise frontier between one form, one color, and another. In his Armenian letters, he uses the word *makur*, meaning "clean." He insisted that firm, dramatic drawing was the basis of painting, and when, during one of the many lost commissions of the 1930s, de Kooning squared up a mural of Gorky's using a series of small delicate strokes, he said "Bill, that's a *mean* way to draw." In that respect, he never changed. Except for a brief moment in 1943, after 1930, there is no painting by Gorky for which there is not at least one, elaborate, "clean" preparatory study, and usually not one, but six or seven.

He gave his paintings titles that evoked the past: *Khorkom*, his village, and the *Enigmatic Combat*, with which, according to an ancient legend, this village had been founded. Yet the first paintings which, as it were, manage to fight their way back from European art to the shores of Lake Van, are the portraits, especially *The Artist and His Mother*, ca. 1926–36 and ca. 1929–42. Both Burkhardt and de Kooning were deeply impressed by these works. Gorky's mother died miserably in her late thirties, and his two versions of her image, painted when Gorky himself was in his late thirties, contain all the words of a conversation that never took place. Through complex coincidence, they continue a tradition of portraiture familiar to David and Ingres, but they are also the first occasion in which Gorky dared to speak about his own childhood.

The later years of the 1930s, by his own account, were bleak and spiritually crushing. Gorky was already becoming a potential recluse. Although his reputation was high, his friends could not see why he made the same painting again and again, on the same canvas, year after year. He seemed to be stuck. When the Second World War broke out, all the preoccupations of the 1930s were overwhelmed by one immense social convulsion. Gorky's reputation, like so many others that had hesitated on the brink of larger recognition, was swept away, forcing him to begin again.

At this point, through de Kooning, Gorky met his second wife, Agnes Magruder, his "Mougouch." A short time later, he met Jeanne Reynal, who immediately bought two paintings from him for more money than he had seen in one check since the Newark Airport murals had been finished, six years earlier. In 1941, through Reynal, a retrospective exhibition was arranged at the San Francisco Museum of Art. Go, said his New York friends. The trip will do you good.

He drove across America with Mougouch and Isamu Noguchi, who was on his way to make some

The Artist and His Mother, ca. 1926–36. Oil on canvas, 60 × 50 inches. Collection Whitney Museum of American Art, New York. Gift of Julien Levy for Maro and Natasha Gorky in memory of their father, 50.17

portrait busts in Hollywood. On a bridge in the middle of the country, Gorky picked a fight with Noguchi as to whether clouds were really clouds, or white horsemen rearing up, clashing fiercely one against the other. Noguchi, who incidentally was also doing the driving, was in favor of letting clouds be clouds. This pragmatism drove Gorky wild: for a moment it seemed as if he were prepared to walk back to Manhattan. Then again, according to Gorky, the mountains of America could never compare to the Caucasus. America, across which he had been chauffeur-driven, was a poor place by comparison!

In San Francisco, a strange city to him, Gorky was impatient with the museum crowd, rude at parties, restless. He tried his hand at sculpture in a borrowed studio, and demolished a block of stone with chisels. He felt no regret toward the sculptor who had loaned him tools and stone, because he was English, and the English had betrayed Armenia. He tried to find somewhere to paint, but succeeded in making only two gouaches. He missed his studio in New York, and suspected that he'd been invited by Noguchi merely to help cover the expenses of the trip. Last, but not least, he got married. In Mougouch, he found a woman sufficiently detached from the art world not to mind the distance he himself was beginning to keep from it. And, she was sufficiently confident, thanks to her own happy East Coast background, to give Gorky a sense of security that otherwise for him was unthinkable.

The expedition to San Francisco cut Gorky's career in half. Just before and after it took place, he was finally beginning to see a way of combining what he had learned, with what he remembered. It required two more new events to get him going: contact with Matta and the other European exiles in New York, who told him that he was old enough and mature enough to be free. Last, but probably foremost, was his prolonged contact with the countryside of Virginia. André Breton's account of the "hybrid" quality of Gorky's art remains the subtlest insight into the workings of this complex mind. Breton saw that in the paintings culled from Loudoun County, Virginia, Gorky at last had placed the imagined orchid from the garden of Khorkom, remembered so clearly, against an example of real luxurious growth, to produce those works which, for this century, are among the finest examples of painting as the art of perception suffused by memory.

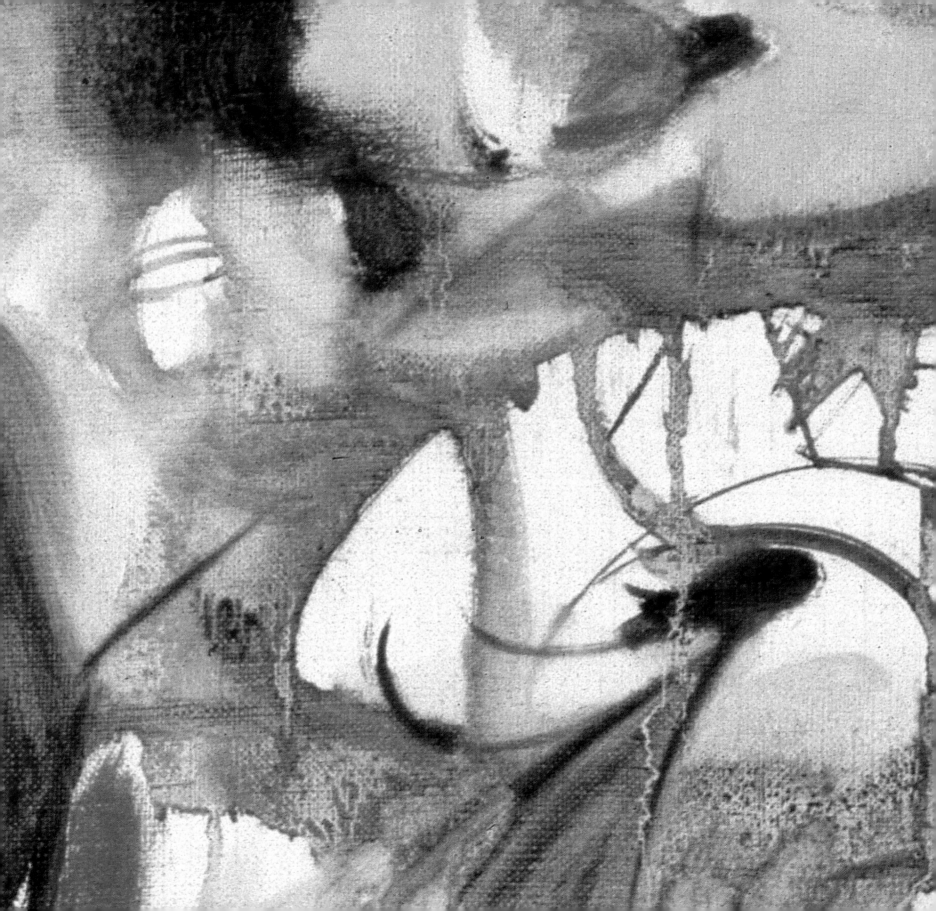

A Straggler's View of Gorky

Dore Ashton

While I was revisiting Gorky, thinking about what could be said given the voluminous commentary already extant, I remembered Baudelaire's apologia for his tardy appreciation of *Madame Bovary*:

> In matters of criticism, the writer who comes after everyone else, the late-comer, has advantages not enjoyed by the writer-prophet, the one who foretells success, who conjures it up, so to speak, by the authority of boldness and devotion.

Baudelaire notes that numerous artists have sung praises of Flaubert's excellent book, and that:

> Nothing therefore remains for criticism to do, but to emphasize a few forgotten points, and to stress a little more vigorously certain traits and highlights that have not, in my view, received their full measure of praise and comment.[1]

The latecomer, Baudelaire says, is a straggler, and is that much more free. While I am not completely a straggler, having at various moments in my working life written about Gorky's painterly riches, I do wish to emphasize "a few forgotten points" and to stress certain traits that have been slighted.

Opposite: Detail, *How My Mother's Embroidered Apron Unfolds in My Life*, 1944. Oil on canvas, 40 × 45 inches. Collection Seattle Art Museum. Gift of Mr. and Mrs. Bagley Wright

I was fortunate to come upon Gorky's late works in the intimate setting of Jeanne Reynal's kitchen while still a student. Reynal, who was both an artist and patron, had done much to sustain Gorky during his last difficult years. (I was surprised to learn later that Reynal, whose internationalist formation was apparent, had been the companion of Boris Anrep, a Russian painter and mosaicist who had also once been the companion of Anna Akhmatova. Perhaps it was easier for Reynal to understand Gorky's complex character than it was for his American colleagues.) What I absorbed, visit by visit, was a drawing, probably of 1947, on a very large scale, in which Gorky had massed small, delicately scored forms that seemed to me to epitomize the organic principle of growth as described by writers from ancient China to Goethe and Klee. In its profuse detail, and subtle absences, that drawing demanded attention of a special kind — the scanner's attention that restlessly moves over and over in order to slowly form a mental ensemble. Another work that hung commandingly in that basement kitchen was uncommonly beautiful, in fact, unforgettable, and reflects, as I now think, one of Gorky's greatest traits: his ability to alter the touch of his brush to accommodate a certain range of feeling. Gently pulsing strokes of ocher and burnt orange and related earth tones unified the surface, pushing back the drama of precisely rendered, yet ambiguous form. I thought then, and still, that Gorky achieved the necessary veil that cloaks the mythical atmosphere he sometimes set out to conjure.

As a straggler, I consider my critical predecessors and remember their reflexive emphasis on Gorky's accumulation of attitudes, gleaned from his close study of both old and modern masters. In their zeal to reveal sources, they have often neglected to convey the wonderful sense of discovery in Gorky's works. When he painted those coursing strokes, probably with a resilient sable brush, allowing the light from behind to peer through only intermittently, his discovery of certain luminous insights in the *act of painting* was no less marvelous than Velasquez's discovery of the mysterious power of pink over a dark ground, or Goya's discovery of the effects of gauzy whites brushed over a pink arm. These sensuous effects, endemic to the art of the oil painter, are more telling than any identification of a Turkish slipper or Armenian plough or Virginia fireplace.

Usually art historians who have studied Gorky closely embark on either one of two rather exclusive paths: the one takes them to Gorky's enthusiasms (usually, as they often fail to stress, of his youth), and his methods of assimilating the lessons of other painters — Cézanne, Picasso, Piero della Francesca, Paolo Uccello, Ingres, and Miró among others — from which they adduce a man who was "a compulsive esthetic ventriloquist"[2] or one who undertook a "series of impersonations".[3] This approach yields a limited idea of the personality of the artist and suggests that only Gorky taught himself by imitation. In fact, many artists of Gorky's generation attempted to emulate modern masters, but they were not as good at it. During the late 1930s, the work of painters showing with the group called American Abstract Artists often looked a lot like Gorky's, and the forms he derived from Picasso or Miró appeared just as often in their works, but with less understanding and intelligence. Gorky's painting intelligence was of a high order, as another remarkable painting intelligence — that of Willem de Kooning — so often insisted. When a painter as young, probably, as twenty-five years old, can pull off an adaptation of synthetic cubism as solid as *Abstraction with Palette*, he is no mere ventriloquist.

The other road — the familiar rubble-strewn road of iconography — has led to just as exclusive (and therefore falsifying) an obsession. In their quest, the iconographers often neglect Gorky's experiments, his byroads, his flexibility, his eye for analogies, and above all, his pleasure in the modifications his practiced brush wrought in the course of painting. Gorky's late preoccupation with his Armenian origins, and the published letters of his last decade, have fueled endless researches into the meaning of certain forms that he favored. The game of identification has its merits, but the one thing it cannot resolve is the perceived meaning of a painting which, to Gorky's lyrical temperament, certainly was polyvalent. Meaning was more an undercurrent, as Coleridge would have said, than a compendium of symbols. I can't agree with the iconographer Harry Rand who believes that you have to understand "the ideational and emotional force behind each shape in Gorky's work"[4] to understand its significance. This flies in the face of Gorky's

Abstraction with Palette, ca. 1930. Oil on canvas, 36 × 48 inches. Collection Philadelphia Museum of Art. Given by Bernard Davis

aesthetics, particularly in his later years, when he sought, above all, to universalize his imagery. The global spirit of universalizing would never admit the pedantry that insists on analyzing each shape for its specificity. Gorky himself always rejected such discrete interpretations, saying he didn't put faces on his forms.

I remember reading in one of Kafka's letters that he believed an artist was a man of many lives, many potential personalities, and many different relationships to his period. Gorky was a man of many lives. He was, at once, a painter who refused to put a face on his forms and a painter who, at times — moved by sentimental memories — assigned associations to certain paintings. When he was being the orphan, the brother, the Armenian waif, so forlorn in an alien world, in his letters to his sister, the Armenian sources were invoked to explain his paintings. But when he was the traveler, along with a dozen or so other painters in New York, on the exciting route to the modern unknown, he was a determined cosmopolitan, rejecting rather haughtily any limiting vision, whether regional or national. And, of course, he was many other things as well, which is why his last works display virtuoso departures from a fixed style. And, why, incidentally, André Breton's often disparaged writings on Gorky are still the finest and most precise entries into his imaginative world. Breton understood the *character* of Gorky's enterprise, and when he wrote that "the eye was not made to take inventory like an auctioneer" but to "cast a lineament, a conducting wire between the most heterogeneous things" he was characterizing Gorky's eye very accurately.[5] Moreover, when Breton ends his introduction with a ringing affirmation of Gorky's ability to "leap beyond the ordinary and the known to indicate, with an impeccable arrow of light, a real feeling of liberty"[6] he speaks of the triumphal nature of Gorky's exhilaration as he repaired to the sunwarmed fields of Virginia to meditate, pencil in hand, on the wealth of form available to the imaginative eye and its natural analogies to human affairs. Breton called him an "eye-spring," and

Gorky with Maro and André Breton, Sherman, Connecticut, Spring 1945. Photograph courtesy Maro Gorky Spender and Matthew Spender

indeed, the sense of original source, the first waters with their cosmogonic implications, flows through Gorky's late drawings and paintings.

II

One of the earliest serious studies of Gorky's oeuvre was undertaken by William C. Seitz, a painter who had moved on to become an art historian, who wisely exclaimed: "What a delicate operation it is to determine what is demonstrably 'there' in a work of art."[7] His discussion, for instance, of the late painting, *The Plow and the Song*, 1947, is more revealing than any biographical or iconographical account could be. For Seitz, Gorky was, in the fullest sense, "a contour draftsman." In his drawings for such works as *The Plow and the Song*:

> ...delineation performs most of its possible functions. Meaning is not in abstraction, but in a painstaking morphology of the visual and tactile world, depicted in a draftsmanship which draws hairline distinctions between fleshy masses, hard bony protuberances, ephemeral clusters of overlapping petals, or the fragile bodies of insects.[8]

Seitz's description of how Gorky worked by a "systematic process" in which he first made line studies, then used the traditional grid method to transfer them to the three canvases, which he thought Gorky worked on alternately, and then filled them in, had been obvious to many writers on Gorky. What distinguishes Seitz's approach is his observation that *everything* in the late Gorky paintings was subject to extreme alteration. He scraped, repainted, and rethought his canvas as he worked. In the same section, Seitz brings in an anecdote — which he uses correctly — to illuminate Gorky's sensuous propensities: around 1945, his friend de Kooning introduced Gorky to the sign painter's so-called "liner brush" which, as Seitz says, Gorky learned how to "trim down to a few hairs" in order to duplicate the free pencil traces in his studies. Gorky thereafter never completely abandoned the marvelously free line this new instrument produced for him. Seitz, in passing, reminds his readers that:

> It is difficult to realize just how little a painter needs, once an idea begins churning in his brain, to start a chain reaction...Gorky could invent a whole cycle of forms from a morphological trait observed in a photograph, in

nature, in a painting of a friend. The same is true of ideas: a word, a phrase, the page of a book read at someone's apartment, or a cue dropped in conversation can set the tone for years of work.[9]

I stress Seitz's approach to Gorky because the best way for the spectator to enter this rich oeuvre is to try to grasp, as Seitz says, just how little a painter needs to start a chain reaction for himself. The entire history of Western paint-

The Plow and the Song, 1947. Oil on burlap, 52 ⅛ × 64 ¼ inches. Private Collection

ing is replete with examples of artists who, in experimenting with the vast possibilities inherent in the medium of oil paint, and, for that matter, pencil, pen, and ink, launched themselves on vertiginous adventures. If one leafs through a book of Rembrandt's sketches, it is obvious that when, in mid-career, he discovered the fluent line — sometimes angular, sometimes shadowed — produced by a reed pen, he leapt into new spaces that surely surprised and delighted him.

III

As Gorky was gathering his forces in his youth, he had many encounters, to which commentators have ascribed various consequences in his work. His birth date has been given either as 1904, 1905, or 1906. If he were born as late as 1906, he was only twenty-four years old in 1930, when he was included in an exhibition at the newly opened Museum of Modern Art in New York and when he installed himself in the famous studio on Union Square. Even if he were already twenty-six, he was still very young as a painter and — given the considerable variety of possibilities in his explorations of diverse modes, both technical and historical — he still had a long way to go. He had been in New York since 1925. Within two years of his arrival in the West Village where he lived on Sullivan Street, he had thoroughly surveyed the methods of the Cubists, as his meticulous drawings of the period attest. By 1930, he was already a teacher of drawing, which would, in itself, demand certain inquiries and a sharpening of his critical approach. To teach, he had to be able to articulate what he himself had learned as he experimented with his pencil and brush. Given his late arrival in the United States — he was already sixteen — and his difficulty with the new language, it is reasonable to assume that he worked hard, for pedagogical reasons, to clarify his ideas about art.

From the late 1920s through the 1930s — crucial years in the development not only of Gorky, but of his painting friends — there are many sightings worth mentioning if only to give some idea of the kaleidoscopic nature of Gorky's undertakings. He met Stuart Davis probably in the fall of 1929, just after Davis had returned from Paris. Gorky spent many hours the following year in the lunch room of the Art Students League where Davis taught and where discussions were always animated. Davis, and the eloquent Russian émigré John Graham, who also quartered himself in the lunchroom, and Gorky became a notable triumvirate. When de Kooning met Gorky, possibly in 1933, he called them "The Three Musketeers." Davis, who was a decade older, and Graham who was still older, were experts on French painting and could offer Gorky advice and information. But whether Gorky always listened seems to me debatable. Quite often, Graham's theoretical writings (which are often incoherent and full of contradictions) are used as a basis to describe Gorky's evolution. But, given the hints in the sightings of Gorky's presence here and there in the various worlds of painters in those days, it is more likely that Gorky, with his avaricious eye and his restless mind, picked up a thread here, a hint there, and then in the fastness of his studio, worked out his own conclusions. It is undeniable that Davis and Gorky made common cause, at least until 1934. Gorky wrote about Davis and Davis about Gorky, and both extolled the modern virtues of Cubism. Gorky admired Davis's succinct statement for his exhibition at the Downtown Gallery in the spring of 1931, in which Davis wrote: "There are an infinite number of form concepts available. My own is very simple and based on the assumption that space is continuous and that matter is discontinuous."[10] Davis also spoke of an idea he called "directional radiation" which, judging by Gorky's work of the period, might very well have activated the latter's imagination. Gorky wrote an appreciation of Davis's work which was published shortly after, in which he referred to Davis's fresh conception of space: "He gives us symbols of tangible spaces, with gravity and physical law," and he praised Davis's catalogue statement in which the artist called his painting "analogical" and spoke about "visual shorthand."[11] Clearly, Gorky shared Davis's aesthetic stance and was greatly stimulated by conversation with the older artist. Gorky continued to speculate about the nature of Cubism and, as late as 1937, tried once again to articulate its program. In a letter to his sister and her family dated July 3, 1937, he states:

> What is the thrust of theoretical cubism? It is to break up the shape of an
> object, to explode it and contract it so as to indicate the fusion of space and
> the object. Cubism implies that space is not empty, that space is alive.
> Whenever an object strikes a two-dimensional surface, the space around the
> object becomes part of that object.[12]

Yet, Gorky also alighted in other milieux, where he would engage in different kinds of conversations. He visited David and Maryusa Burliuk, whose Russian vanguard credentials appealed to him. The Burliuks sustained an informal salon where a samovar stood always ready, and where other Russian-born artists, such as the Soyer twins, Raphael and Moses, participated in long, sometimes heated arguments about life, the world, and even art. Other places Gorky was known to frequent provided different stimuli. He was a steady customer, or at least visitor, at Weyhe's bookstore on Lexington Avenue where he and most of his friends were able to keep up with the latest periodicals and art books from Europe. An inveterate browser, Gorky supplemented Graham's firsthand information about shifts in vanguard thought in Paris (Graham also shared his copies of such French periodicals as *Cahiers d'Art, XXième Siècle*, and *Documents*, as well as Surrealist publications, with many artists) with glances at other publications. He obviously paid attention to articles in which such between-the-wars tendencies as new classicism appeared. Not only did he show considerable interest in Giorgio de Chirico, but certain drawings and paintings show that he knew about the other artists in the Italian classicizing movement known as *Valori Plastici*, and also, about such Parisian shifts as evidenced in the work of Derain. In the viscid paint and rhythmic brushing in several Gorky still lifes, such as a still life dated around 1928, and two flower paintings of about ten years later, Derain's style is evidently studied. And then, there were other vanguard spirits with whom Gorky would intermittently meet, such as Frederick Kiesler, the indefatigable Austrian vanguardist who buzzed around various artistic circles preaching radical aesthetic views, Buckminster Fuller, and Max Weber, who had once studied with Matisse, and who could be found in the lunchroom at the Art Students League. There were scores of others, who at various times, were important to Gorky.

As for the evolution of Gorky's views on the meaning of art, there is reason to assume that there were several important sources, among them John Dewey, whose ideas were frequently discussed by painters of Gorky's acquaintance, and several of the Surrealists. Dewey's advocacy of art as "lived" experience was a powerful force. Even when Davis wrote hortatively, explaining the importance of the Artists' Union, he leaned on Dewey to explain the social function of the artist: "A work of art is a public act, or, as John Dewey says, an 'experience'."[13] A few years later, Dewey was still frequently cited by artists in Gorky's circle. Matta, who would become a significant sounding board for Gorky, was impressed by Dewey's ideas, most particularly the notion of the organic, or dynamic, growing principle at the heart of the aesthetic experience. He was well prepared to accept Dewey's thesis since the Surrealists, whom Matta had encountered before he left France in 1939, entertained parallel views. When Julien Levy published his book *Surrealism* in 1936 — a book Levy claimed was closely studied by Gorky — it was not only the first book in English on that high moment of collaborative literary and artistic activity, but also the first introduction of the French philosopher, Gaston Bachelard, to an English-reading public. Bachelard's burgeoning aesthetic concerning the function of the imagination was, in many ways, comparable to Dewey's. His attack on the purely logical approach to experience was spirited. He said that "in the domain of thought imprudence is a method" and that "a psychic revolution has surely just occurred in this century; human reason has just weighed anchor; the spiritual voyage has begun and consciousness has left the shores of immediate reality."[14]

Levy's gallery had been open since 1932 and was one of Gorky's regular haunts. There, he not only saw works by the major Surrealist painters, but also the various small publications they busily produced all during the 1920s and 1930s. But it was not until Levy's book that Gorky could familiarize himself with the work of the key Surrealist poets. He was clearly elated with the discovery of Paul Eluard, deftly translated by Samuel Beckett, and promptly appropriated "Lady Love" by Eluard for use in a love letter. It is not hard to imagine Gorky's attraction to Eluard above all — Eluard who spoke always of vision, eyes, vast skies, and sky colors, Eluard, the most tender of the surrealizing poets. But it was not only Eluard Gorky found in Levy's book. Beckett had translated passages from André Breton himself, from "Soluble Fish," one of his most delirious poems, and from "The White Haired Revolver" written in 1932, including such visual images as a statue of Lautrêamont, and a glass case containing "a prong of lightning." No doubt Gorky also entered the spirit of Picasso's poem of 1935, in which the artist runs on at breakneck pace and without punctuation in a cascade of free associations.

I believe there were two Surrealist preoccupations that engaged Gorky's imagination in the later 1930s: the first was certainly the technique of visual free association advocated by all the Surrealist theorists who always appreciated close study of morphological and metamorphic detail. The stress on organic form found so often in Surrealist writers was later supplemented for New York artists by their perusal of D'Arcy Wentworth Thompson's *On Growth and Form*, a monumental study published in 1942 and reprinted in 1952. The second Surrealist preoccupation that Gorky responded to was the heightened interest in the arts of primitive and non-Western societies and early periods in European art. Gorky and other painters who would later be called Abstract Expressionists had only to turn the pages of *Documents* edited by Georges Bataille, several issues of which Gorky owned, or *Cahiers d'Art* or *Minotaure* to see illustrations for numerous anthropological or art historical articles on either extremely ancient art or contemporary ethnic art, to which they appended "primitive" European painting, most particularly that of Uccello.

I don't think it possible to chronicle all of Gorky's imaginative wanderings as he trod the streets of Manhattan during the 1930s, or his quarrels, reconciliations, associations. But surely, as a prelude to his final years as a practicing artist, the artistic events of the period must be mentioned. First of all, the procession of extraordinary exhibitions that Alfred Barr mounted with the express purpose of elucidating modern movements. New Yorkers had the rare privilege (which even the Europeans had not) of seeing large compendia of stylistically related works. In 1936 alone, there was *Cubism and Abstract Art* in the spring, and *Fantastic Art, Dada and Surrealism* in the late fall. Both Pierre Matisse and Julien Levy had already frequently shown the major Surrealist painters and would continue to disseminate catalogues and other publications for years to come. Picasso's works were exhibited regularly in New York and assiduously collected by The Museum of Modern Art. When the Spanish civil war incited Picasso to paint *Guernica*, the large painting was soon after shipped to New York where it became a point of repair for artists, and was closely examined by Gorky, always a reverent and intelligent admirer of the Spanish master.

IV

Toward the late 1930s, artists of Gorky's acquaintance, and he himself, began to take a great interest in the character of ancient myths. This interest, of course, had preoccupied Breton, who always had a great penchant for seeing purer and more vivid meanings in the arts of the most distant past. In some cases (Still, Newman, Pollock), this faith in the expressive superiority of temporarily distant origins, as expressed in either ancient or "primitive" contemporary art, led to an inquiry into native American sources, which Breton himself had long cherished. Others — Rothko for instance, who apparently had once briefly studied with Gorky — turned back to ancient Greek or near-Eastern sources. From what we know about Gorky's earlier interest, it seems to me that Gorky's own conscious turning toward myth arrived at about the same time. He had had long

Garden in Sochi, 1941. Oil on canvas, 44 ¼ × 62 ¼ inches. Collection The Museum of Modern Art, New York. Purchase Fund and gift of Mr. and Mrs. Wolfgang S. Schwabacher (by exchange)

experience in creating personal myths, as numerous accounts of his idiosyncracies, his prevarications, his deliberate invocations of his Armenian heritage in terms of song, food, and dress (which Davis always suspected of being egotistic bids for attention) indicated. Just about when his colleagues took their mythology turning to ancient horizons, Gorky took his own. Since he had the advantage of a singularly remote background, it was natural enough to set himself apart by turning back to his native Armenia. "The real treasure, the treasure that brings our wretchedness and our ordeals to an end, is never far away," wrote Heinrich Zimmer. "We must never go looking for it in distant lands, for it lies buried in the most secret recesses of our own house."[15] Gorky undertook his conscious search in his own house around 1937, when he wrote to his sister that he was "fascinated by the universality of art,"[16] explaining that he sometimes paints a thought or concept and then sees the very same one for the first time in some ancient work of art. Then, perhaps because it was to his sister and her family he was writing, he adds a few sentences attaching his idea to ancient Armenian sources. Probably, around 1938, he began dredging up childhood memories expressly to inspire his work, delighting in embellishing them, much like the ancient Armenian illuminators, with colorful detail. His painting with the title of his hometown, *Khorkom*, points the way to effusive mythologizing, of which the often cited note of June 1942, to The Museum of Modern Art concerning *Garden in Sochi*, is a prime example.[17] Gorky's lyrical temperament — he had begun writing poems at an early age — emerges in full flower once he enlisted his childhood memories from distant Lake Van in his work. I have no doubt that his attention to the free association practiced by Surrealist poets limbered up his imagination. Also, the permissions implied in Picasso's Surrealist poetry published in the 1930s in *Cahiers d'Art* and partially cited in various English translations thereafter, spurred Gorky's lyrical impulses that operated primarily in his way of poeticizing forms in nature — that is, elaborating metaphors and analogies visually. This method appeared simultaneously in his drawings and his poems, which, written after the 1939 Picasso exhibition, and Alfred Barr's book, sound very much like Picasso's most surrealist utterances. The prototype of Gorky's mythologizing statement on the *Garden in Sochi*, written in June 1942, is first offered in a poem written about a year earlier. "Duty of Water",[18] begins:

> Move us to the cool chalk-like what clarity
> over all tortures where once great centuries
> danced celtic with gaiety bleeds on they mouth
> of me in paradises
> apricots shape apricots dependent breasts
> deprived of leaves was the Holy. Tree of their
> clothes banners under pressure to the sh-h-h-sh-h
> isle of Manhattan

The poem alludes to colors in a painter's way as does Picasso, in phrases such as: "becomes green is black" and "white chalk white angels black angels move."

In fact, Gorky, while retrieving his early memories, was at the same time revisiting his artistic sources in modern art, to which he was always faithful. His shuttling back and forth, remembering forms or themes as the occasion required, was not unlike the way other painters functioned, and certainly his study of the first major retrospective of Picasso at The Museum of Modern Art refreshed his memory. Proof lies in his drawings in which he goes back to Picasso's 1933 drawing called *An Anatomy*, and the drawings for a monument reproduced in Barr's book. Gorky had apparently first studied Picasso's sculpturesque drawings of bonelike shapes in 1931 and recapitulated the themes in an ink drawing of 1941. Not only did he reexamine Picasso in his drawings of 1941–42, he even made provisory gouache sketches for a mural based directly on Picasso's "Lysistrata" illustrations.

At the same time, his fealty to Miró was reaffirmed. Miró was even closer to Gorky's sensibility and always maintained that his painting had more to do with poetry than with painting. Golding puts it nicely when he says that Gorky had certain "elective affinities" with the Surrealist movement, and suggests that Miró's interest in Catalan and folk art "must have struck affinities with Gorky's newly aroused consciousness of his Armenian heritage."[19] Golding rightly says that Miró's influence hit Gorky "most squarely" between 1940 and 1944 (the large Miró retrospective at The Museum of Modern Art was in 1941). But the affinities are even more startling if we take into account Gorky's "looking into the grass" which begins as far as I can tell with his trips to Connecticut in 1942, his sojourn at David Hare's house in Roxbury, Connecticut, two years after, and his prolonged visits to his wife's family farm in Virginia beginning in 1943. Miró, writing from Montroig in Catalonia in 1916, where he'd gone to "live with the landscape" and to "ennoble myself at this sight. . . I love every tiny creature, every blade of grass" would exclaim in 1918, "What happiness to comprehend a single blade of grass in a landscape."[20] This sentiment, according to James Johnson Sweeney, who spoke with Gorky about his work in 1944, captures the precise nature of Gorky's satisfaction in his works from around 1942 on.[21]

Much art historical wrangling has occurred around the issue of how much, if, or from whom, Gorky's surrealist tendency derived, and most particularly, whether the arrival of a large contingent of the Parisian crew during the Second World War had a great or minimal impact on him. I think that it is obvious that a man of Gorky's visual curiosity, which led to perpetual inquisition of works of art, would naturally take an interest in the artists who made them. Long before such artists as André Masson or Yves Tanguy, or Miró himself, appeared in New York, Gorky had studied their work in exhibitions and publications. Matthew Spender suggests that a reproduction of Masson's mural sketch in *Documents #5*, 1930, might have inspired Gorky's forms in an important series of drawings in the early 1930s most often described as Picasso-derived.[22] Gorky would surely have seen Masson's ink drawings that were repeatedly exhibited, usually supplemented with elegant little catalogues, at Curt Valentin's Gallery. Masson's early colleague, Yves Tanguy — they had known each other well from the 1920s — might have been even more important for Gorky, judging by Gorky's drawings. Tanguy arrived in America in 1940, lived briefly near Matta in Manhattan, and then removed himself to Connecticut, as had Masson, Calder, Levy, and eventually, Gorky. Levy had shown Tanguy's drawings, paintings, and gouaches in 1936, but even before, Gorky could have seen them reproduced in *Documents*. Toward the mid-1930s, Tanguy produced a number of incisive ink drawings in which there were hybrid forms. There, Gorky could see bonelike members that fit together like ceramic plumbing pipes, elliptical platforms that stand for human pelvises, cocoonlike shapes, and standing figures with hair stylized into points — features that can be found in Gorky's own drawings. When *View*, founded in 1940, featured an issue on Tanguy in May 1942, the drawings most certainly bore a familiar air for Gorky.

Then, there is the vexing question of Matta's influence. Matta, the youngest and newest convert to Breton's views, arrived in New York at the outbreak of the war and remained for several years. Gorky met him in 1940 and was immediately drawn to the charming, voluble, and energetic young convert. Critics who see an "influence" from the younger and perhaps more cosmopolitan painter refer usually to Gorky's softening of contours and his more pointed allusion to multiple spaces. As a straggler, I would point out that Matta himself, who had only been painting for two or three years, had absorbed certain influences in Paris, where he knew the circle in which Kandinsky was admired. Matta's drawings in pencil and crayon shortly before he left Europe, and during his first years in New York, bear great resemblance to Kandinsky's drawings. Floating markers of color — what Ethel Schwabacher called "plumes" in Gorky's drawings of the 1940s — were used by Kandinsky to suggest various points in a virtually global space, as were swirling lines, blank shapes, and occasional representational details wrenched from their customary forms. Kandinsky's work, so profusely represented in The Solomon R. Guggenheim Collection of Non-Objective Paintings, was available to New York artists from the late 1930s, and, in 1945 was mounted in a commemorative exhibition. Gorky appreciated Kandinsky's audacity with color detached from its descriptive functions, and in one of his most magnificent paintings, *The Liver is the Cock's Comb*, 1944 (which

I think of almost as an homage) Gorky remembers Kandinsky (in the crimsons and blacks particularly).

Matta's close friend, Gordon Onslow-Ford, who arrived in New York around the same time, was a zealous broadcaster of Surrealist principles and, in 1941, at the New School for Social Research gave a series of lectures on Surrealism that were attended by several artists who were later called Abstract Expressionists. No doubt it was Matta who brought Gorky and who, at least in 1941, excited Gorky's curiosity about the possibilities inherent in the exercise of automatism. But, Matta's presence was also coincidental with Gorky's new thoughts about landscape, and in a reminiscence of the period, Matta speaks about things that certainly would have found a warm response in Gorky who was arriving at the same place, more or less, on his own. "When I arrived in the United States," Matta told an interviewer, "I started talking about the earth...the earth as something terrific, burning, changing, transforming, growing." He talked about Gorky affectionately, saying, "I felt very close to Gorky. You know, he was an Andalusian man, he sang songs and looked at the flowers."[23]

All of the encounters that can be sighted in accounts of Gorky's artistic development can be given differing weights, as the criticism shows, but by around 1940, when Gorky was still in his mid-thirties — a relatively young age for a serious painter — they had been translated into mere echoes in an oeuvre that begins to take on a clear, idiosyncratic character.

V

When Breton said that Gorky "treated nature as a cryptogram," he did not mean that this roving eye-spring, Gorky, painted for cryptographers. What Breton understood was the nature of Gorky's temperament, the lyrical temperament that always sees with an eye for internal rhymes. And, free associations. Poetic rhyming, on the paper or canvas surface can emerge either as figures, geometric or organic; as colors, naturalistic or imagined; or as spaces, sensed rather than pictured. Analogy occurs in the working. Perhaps Julien Levy was right to mention an anecdote (so often anecdotes are presumptuous) in which he told Gorky about Paul Eluard's working method, quoting the poet: "I hum a melody, some popular song, the most ordinary. Sometimes I sing quite loudly. But I echo very softly in my interior, filling the melody with my own errant words."[24] Gorky himself remarked that when you watch children, they talk to themselves as they draw, indicating continuous inner association, saying this is a house, this is a dog, and so on. And Gorky's friend de Kooning said you can start with anything to get your imagination in shape (one of the few Surrealist methods that de Kooning absorbed) and sometimes started a painting with a simple letter from the alphabet, or a number. One of the many writers on Gorky intent on identifying Gorky's exact meanings thought he had found the answers in one of the late paintings: "In *The Calendars*, Gorky," he wrote, "used color first to identify a shape for himself and then to confuse the viewer with a repetition of the same shape in an illogical but formally pleasing location."[25] Confuse the viewer? But the first viewer of the lyrical artist is himself, and he is not looking for confusion but consonance. Or, the completion of a feeling, a work. What characterizes the late paintings is Gorky's willingness to shift gears. He found many different forms and techniques to evoke differing emotional climates — scumbling, masking, scraping, shifting perspectives, antique ways of making small and large relative, spotlighting, darkening corners — all in the service of generalized or diffused feelings. In his late works, Gorky was still faithful to principles drawn from his study of early modern art. "It is better to be conscientiously troubled and perplexed by the vastness of the unknown, than content with the little that is known," he wrote in 1940.[26] And in 1944: "When I now speak of place, I do not mean a static condition of equilibrium where all elements have been finally organized and framed."[27]

To keep his canvas alive, and open to fortuitous suggestions as he worked, Gorky often recapitulated motifs from one canvas to another, or even techniques. A great deal of significance has been posited in his adoption of turpentine-thinned paint in the early 1940s, and it seems that Matta claimed to have advised Gorky on this point. But, Gorky always held visual experiences he had had in reserve, and when he needed a means to express certain feelings, he drew upon them. Miró's own use of thinned, running paint in an early work owned by The Museum of Modern Art, *The Birth of the World*, 1925, probably derived from the same intuitive need. If nature were the source of *Waterfall*, 1942–43, with its thinned, dripping greens, and its lightly scumbled surfaces, and if the whitened surfaces were indeed the light on rushing water, then certainly Gorky had needed the rills to suggest flickering movement. The same can be said for a painting of 1944, *One Year the Milkweed*, in which the sliding washes move downwards, producing a scrim through which discrete forms produce a "place" that is never static. One might detect chrysalides, cocoons, milkweed, drifting in this atmosphere, but one visits the surface with the erratic motion of a fly, and from no fixed position. How Gorky could shift in feeling can be seen if two paintings from the same year are considered: the masterwork *The Liver is the Cock's Comb* and *How My Mother's Embroidered Apron Unfolds in My Life*. The

How My Mother's Embroidered Apron Unfolds in My Life, 1944. Oil on canvas, 40 × 45 inches. Collection Seattle Art Museum. Gift of Mr. and Mrs. Bagley Wright

Liver is replete with lovingly drawn details suggesting claws, feathers, organs, taking their places in vertiginously shifting spaces painted with brio in short strokes that produce a vibrato on differing levels in space. *How My Mother's Embroidered Apron Unfolds in My Life* is figured with similar shapes, but they are blurred, made ambiguous by thin trails of color that fuse rather than vibrate, soften rather than heighten. Over the years, Gorky had developed a horde of images, or sometimes just suggestive shapes, on which he could draw as the spirit moved him. This reservoir of shapes is not to be confused with symbols.

Both de Kooning, who often talked of expressive shapes, and who, like Gorky, could spot them anywhere — in a newspaper photograph, in the street, even in the comic strips — and Gorky himself, cherished the visual character of the unusual shape for its own expressive self and not necessarily as symbolizing some *thing* else.

I think it is safe to say that Gorky had understood his own impulses quite well by 1944, when he wrote a long letter to his sister in which he described his idea of the organization of space:

> It is an organization of agitating points or places or locations. These points
> can exist in my concept of color, they can consist in taking a shape. Now try to
> allow your mind the freedom to think in terms of constant motion or flux
> instead of paralysis. Replace stillness with movement. That is my goal, that is
> what I am achieving. I am breaching the static barrier, penetrating rigidity. I
> am destroying confinement of the inert wall to achieve fluidity, motion,
> warmth in expressing feelingness, the pulsation of nature as it throbs.[28]

Gorky was breaching the static barrier by 1941 in *Garden in Sochi* in which, by subtle articulation of his impasto, he played with rhyming shapes in deliberately ambiguous space. There are already several levels of space, and shapes are fashioned by masking out in order to create what used to be called negative spaces. By the time he met both Breton and Miró in 1944, Gorky had a clear idea of the direction he wanted to take, and it pleased both of his new acquaintances, who knew how to read Gorky's impulses.

When Gorky speaks of "warmth in expressing feelingness," I think his troubador's nature is evident. What the "feelingness" is about is open to various responses. It is not impossible that the vignetted form at the upper left (the vignette was a favored method to suggest the levels in space as well as the compartmented nature of experiences) of the destroyed painting, *The Calendars*, is a seated female nude. In fact, such an association is unavoidable once a large group of drawings in which the form appears is studied. She is there quite literally, with breasts decisively delineated in another painting of the same time, *The Betrothal* and its sister, *The Betrothal II*. But she is also there in far more ambiguous form in the lightly painted, airy *Making the Calendar*. In *The Betrothal*, Gorky uses the breasts in their insert at upper left almost as a key-signature in music. The other forms, echoing, are far less specific, and suggest organically growing things with one of Gorky's favorite devices — darkened centers within the forms that are like the nucleus of living cells. Both in the Yale and the Whitney *Betrothals*, Gorky works to sustain warmth, "feelingness" with virtuoso passages of color. He used relatively rough-grained canvas, but he built up or scraped down, so that warm sequences of color — ochers over greens, blues impinging on violets over reds — would heighten the expression of a bright, emotionally satisfying place in which heartfelt inner events take place.

I've always found it tedious to read written exegeses of paintings, and I don't intend to analyze Gorky's late works inch-by-inch. I believe it is sufficient to stress that what Gorky achieved in those last years of his young life was not just a rich vocabulary of forms, but a range of techniques as well. Many of the late drawings reveal him inventing new means to get at "the feelingness" of things. Some of the charcoal drawings are made articulate by rubbing out. Some of the crayon and pencil drawings are visibly scraped with a razor to suggest the air invading specific shapes. A lot can be guessed at just by observing when Gorky takes a motif and draws it in a horizontal format and then takes the same motif into a vertical format. Landscape or figure? Nature or human nature? He was after both. Often the individual forms are read by means of Gorky's titles, but I don't think too much weight should be put on them, as he himself said on several occasions. Like his friends among the Surrealists (for even if Gorky eventually rejected Surrealism, he remained a friend to Surrealists, and never renounced certain basic tenets of the movement), Gorky could invent differing associations for the same image on different occasions. His paintings should be read much more indulgently than by keying them to the words of the title.

VI

Seitz says that "like a mystic or a philosopher, Gorky glimpsed an ideal reality. His unknown center lay both outside and within his personality."[29] He then quotes Gorky from a letter that Ethel Schwabacher showed him:

> I am an individual — Gorky — and it is my individual feeling which counts the most. Why? I do not know nor do I wish to know. I accept it as a fact which does not need explanation.[30]

Although Gorky did not wish to know, a lot of other individuals were most eager to know, and there has been a growing literature on him in which the facts of his life, the circumstances of his youth, and his tragic end, have sponsored a lot of psychologizing and pontificating. This is a very hazardous path to the truth of his paintings, for, as I said in the beginning, most artists live many lives. But their fullest life is within the work, and that is where we must forage for their truths. If there are two currents — continuity and discontinuity — in twentieth-century art, as I have always believed, then Gorky probably represents continuity. He had a sense of tradition. But what tradition? It is tempting, in view of the late letters about Armenia, to believe that it was his personal tradition, as experienced in ancient Armenian churches as a child, or as learned at his mother's knee. But I think Gorky's work is markedly in the modern tradition, which at least at mid-century, sustained not only the romance of the artist who sacrifices everything to Art, but also, the romance of the unknown, and the importance of intense probing, which entails risk.

Recognition of tragedy is also part of that tradition, and there is no doubt that Gorky carried not only his personal tragedy, which included memories of a holocaust, but also the tragedy of his people, in his heart. But what is the measure of such immense sorrow? Gorky was both a witness and a victim of a holocaust. Perhaps as a result, he could experience heightened emotions. Perhaps he also had a keener sense of an anterior paradise. Perhaps his extreme emotionality was nurtured by dim memories of terror. He seemed to think so. Yet, in the broadest perspective of his life's work, these increments in his formation are not identifiable. He wandered in his most youthful works in various traditions — all rehearsals for his great ambition, which was to be Gorky. When everyone was seeking origins in distant temporal, even millenial horizons, Gorky, too, was searching. One of his close friends during the period of his most realized works, from the late 1930s until his death, was the sculptor Isamu Noguchi, who, like Gorky, did not feel at home in his home, America, and who, like Gorky, was strongly attracted to the hybrid worlds produced by Surrealist thought. Noguchi reported that he and Gorky on their junkets to the Metropolitan Museum of Art, or in their visits to each other's studios, often spoke of their feelings of alienation, their separateness from the very milieu that nurtured their talent. Noguchi, too, bore witness to the devastation of a people, with whom part of him identified, in Hiroshima and Nagasaki. But he, too, when his life's work is surveyed, avoided overt references to his inner sadness.

My late friend, the composer Morton Feldman, used to say that some of his music was a kind of mourning, but he would never say of what. Probably the mourning that Gorky expressed in his letters evaporated as he worked, as the joys of shaping matter took him in their thrall. In his many lives, this complicated artist may have dissembled, as we know he did in his love letters, and as his early claims of Russian heritage suggest, but in his works there are other values, and truth, I think, was his greatest lure: truth to his experience, to his "feelingness"; to his being Gorky, an individual; to his love of beauty. The facts, the real facts of his inner life, are his paintings.

1. Charles Baudelaire, "*Madame Bovary* by Gustave Flaubert" in *Selected Writings on Art and Literature* (New York: Penguin Books USA, 1972), p. 244.

2. Robert Storr, "Fertile Mirrors" in *Arshile Gorky: 1904-1948* (Madrid: Fundacion Caja de Pensiones and London: Whitechapel Art Gallery, 1989), p. 27.

3. John Golding, "Arshile Gorky: The Search for Self" in *Arshile Gorky: 1904-1948*, p.15.

4. Harry Rand, *Arshile Gorky: The Implications of Symbols* (Montclair, N.J.: Allenheld, Osmun & Co., Publishers, Inc., and London: George Prior Associated Publishers Ltd., 1981), p. 54.

5. André Breton, "The Eye-Spring: Arshile Gorky" in *Arshile Gorky* (New York: Julien Levy Gallery, March 1945), n.p. Also quoted in Julien Levy, *Arshile Gorky* (New York: Harry N. Abrams, Inc., 1966), p. 34.

6. Ibid.; Also quoted in Levy, p. 20.

7. Quoted in Dore Ashton, "Introduction" in William C. Seitz, *Abstract Expressionist Painting in America* (Cambridge, Mass. and London, England: Harvard University Press for the National Gallery of Art, 1983), p. xvi.

8. Seitz, *Abstract Expressionist Painting in America*, p. 16.

9. Ibid., p. 160.

10. *Stuart Davis* (New York: The Downtown Gallery, 1931).

11. Arshele Gorky, "Stuart Davis," *Creative Art* (New York), September 1931, p. 213.

12. Letter to Vartoosh, Moorad, and Karlen Mooradian, July 3, 1937, in Karlen Mooradian, "A Special Issue on Arshile Gorky," *Ararat* (New York), Fall 1971, p. 20.

13. Stuart Davis, "The Artist Today," *American Magazine of Art* (New York), August 1935, p. 506.

14. Gaston Bachelard, "Surrationalism" in Julien Levy, *Surrealism* (New York: The Black Sun Press, 1936), pp. 188-89.

15. Heinrich Zimmer, quoted in Mircea Eliade, *Symbolism, The Sacred and the Arts*, ed. Diane Apostolos (New York: Crossroad, ca. 1985), p. 94.

16. Letter to Vartoosh, Moorad, and Karlen Mooradian, July 3, 1937, in *Ararat*, p. 20.

17. Reprinted in Ethel K. Schwabacher, *Arshile Gorky* (New York: The Macmillan Company for the Whitney Museum of American Art, 1957), p.66.

18. Golding, p. 20.

19. Ibid., p.19.

20. Jacques Dupin, *Miró* (New York: Harry N. Abrams, Inc., 1962), pp. 65 and 83. Also quoted in Dore Ashton, "Stripping Down to Cosmos" in *A Reading of Modern Art* (New York: Harper & Row, 1971), p. 54.

21. James Johnson Sweeney, "Five American Painters," *Harper's Bazaar* (New York), April 1944, p.122.

22. Matthew Spender, "Origines et Développement de l'oeuvre dessiné de Arshile Gorky" in *Arshile Gorky: Oeuvres sur Papier 1929-1947* (Lausanne: Musée Cantonal des Beaux-Arts Lausanne, 1990), p. 21.

23. Nancy Miller, "Interview with Matta" in *Matta: The First Decade* (Waltham, Mass.: Rose Art Museum, Brandeis University, 1982), p. 15.

24. Golding, p. 20.

25. Rand, *Arshile Gorky: The Implications of Symbols*, p. 125.

26. Letter to Vartoosh Mooradian, November 24, 1940, in *Ararat*, p. 25.

27. Letter to Vartoosh Mooradian, February 14, 1944, in *Ararat*, p. 31.

28. Ibid.

29. Seitz, p. 133.

30. Ibid.

An Erotic Garden

MICHAEL AUPING

WHEN SIDNEY JANIS WAS NEGOTIATING the sale of Arshile Gorky's *The Liver is the Cock's Comb*, 1944, he told Seymour H. Knox that "Gorky felt this was his ultimate statement, but worried about getting it into a museum. He knew it was a little erotic."[1] Janis's enthusiasm for *The Liver* can be dismissed as the promotional language often used to make a major sale. On the other hand, the physical evidence — that is, the powerful presence and effect of the painting itself — remains a testament to Janis's adulation and his description regarding the work's sensual character.

Every great artist has a particularly concentrated moment of creative energy where experience, experimentation, and ambition come together to forge a pinnacle expression. Cézanne's *Bathers*, 1906; Matisse's *The Dance*, 1909–10; Picasso's *Guernica*, 1937, or Pollock's great *One: Number 31*, 1950, are examples of such moments in the twentieth century. Within Gorky's oeuvre, *The Liver* plays a similar role. Completed in 1944, it stands at the heart of Gorky's breakthrough years. Between 1942 and 1947, the artist created his most daring images, and *The Liver* both summarizes what came before it and announces the deep levels of content that would fill the imagery of his remaining years. Specifically, it declares the fundamentally erotic character of Gorky's vision of nature.

Opposite: Detail, *The Liver is the Cock's Comb*, 1944. Oil on canvas, 73 $^{1}/_{4}$ × 98 inches. Collection Albright-Knox Art Gallery, Buffalo, New York. Gift of Seymour H. Knox, 1956

Painted during a year that produced many of Gorky's masterpieces — *How My Mother's Embroidered Apron Unfolds in My Life*, 1944; *One Year the Milkweed*, 1944; *Water of the Flowery Mill*, 1944 — *The Liver* was sold immediately upon completion to his friend and patron Jean Hebbeln. It would have been the centerpiece of what was arguably the most important exhibition in Gorky's lifetime — a one-person exhibition at Julien Levy Gallery in 1945 — but Levy thought that only pictures for sale should be included.[2] An essay accompanying the checklist was authored by the French Surrealist poet André Breton. Often reserved in his assessment of American art, Breton announced that Gorky had singularly discovered "the secret," and it was *The Liver* that resoundingly announced this fact to Breton. Although *The Liver* was not included in the exhibition, Breton had seen it in Gorky's studio, and it is the only work expressly singled out in his text. According to the poet, ". . . 'The Liver is the Cock's Comb'. . .should be considered the great open door to the analogy world."[3] The Surrealists trafficked regularly in the analogical world, where no image remained constant, but underwent a perpetual mutation of form and meaning. Likewise, in Gorky's complex vision, nature and self, memory and immediate perception, body and imagination, became inextricably intertwined, creating an often complex symbolic structure.

Like all of the artist's mature paintings, *The Liver* presents a "collaged" field of organic, biomorphic, and abstract forms. Enigmatic symbols and ideographic shapes cover the surface of the canvas, setting up multiple references. As a result, the distinction between subject matter — the psychological and/or narrative content of an image — and object matter — a depicted scene or object — is one of the most intriguing aspects of Gorky's work of the 1940s; this distinction is particularly apparent in *The Liver*. During the 1940s, it can be said that Gorky's object matter was primarily landscape, often drawn directly from nature at Crooked Run Farm, the home of his parents-in-law in Virginia. Gorky's subject matter, however — the way he internalized what he saw and reinvented to create analogies for his own preoccupations and fantasies — is a more complex issue.

Having spent his adult life as an artist in New York, studying art in museums, Gorky's engagement with nature in the 1940s stimulated a new sense of experimentation, not only with what he was painting, but also with how he would paint

The Liver is the Cock's Comb, 1944. Oil on canvas, 73 ¼ × 98 inches. Collection Albright-Knox Art Gallery, Buffalo, New York. Gift of Seymour H. Knox, 1956

it. The result was a peculiar fusion of intense visual observation and abstract fantasy. Describing Gorky's works of 1943–44, James Johnson Sweeney wrote:

> Arshile Gorky's latest work shows his realization of the value of literally return-ing to the earth . . . . Last summer Gorky decided to "look into the grass" as he put it. The product was a series of monumentally drawn details of what one might see in the heavy August grass.[4]

Gorky was a consummate draftsman who developed numerous studies of his observations using an exceptionally fine-pointed pencil and crayons. Observing nature for hours at a time, his intense meditations resulted in dynamic clusters of images that fused, in his mind and on paper, observed reality and imagina-tion. These clusters, which began to develop specific meanings for Gorky, were often fitted into the compositions of larger paintings.

Gorky's engagement with nature was reinforced by his appreciation of the work of Kandinsky and Miró, and, in many respects, *The Liver* is a grand summation of the work of these modern pioneers of abstraction and Surrealism. Gorky's admiration for Kandinsky led him to claim falsely that he had studied abroad with the Russian artist for three months in 1920.[5] Gorky was particularly inspired by Kandinsky's early landscapes and his ability to meld childhood memories with nature-inspired imagery. Kandinsky's autobiography, *Rückblicke* which Gorky is likely to have read, refers to this process.[6] Nature also represented poignant childhood memories for Gorky; eventually, powerful mythical and allegorical symbols would be evident as well. In 1942, he wrote to his sister Vartoosh:

> Sweet Vartoosh, loving memories of our garden in Armenia's Khorkom haunt me frequently. Recall Father's garden down the path from our house and the Tree of the Cross upon which the authentic Armenian villagers attached the colorful pennants of their clothing. Within our garden could be found the glorious and living panoply of Armenian nature, so unknown to all yet so in need of being known. Beloved sister, in my art I often draw our garden and recreate its precious greenery and life. Can a son forget the soil which sires him?

> Beloveds, the stuff of thought is the seed of the artist. Dreams form the bristles of the artist's brush. And as the eye functions as the brain's sentry, I communicate my most private perceptions through art, my view of the world. In trying to probe beyond the ordinary and the known, I create an inner infinity. I probe within the confines of the finite to create an infinity. Liver. Bones. Living rocks and living plants and animals. Living dreams. Vartoosh dearest, to this I owe my debt to our Armenian art. Its hybrids, its many opposites. The inventions of our folk imagination. These I attempt to capture directly, I mean the folklore and physical beauty of our homeland, in my works.[7]

Gorky also read Kandinsky's book *Concerning the Spiritual in Art* and was familiar with Kandinsky's philosophy that analogy could be achieved between colors and emotions. Color became increasingly important to Gorky in the 1940s, and it is in relation to color that *The Liver* is such a grand statement. Gorky was essentially an easel painter, yet *The Liver* is by far the largest of Gorky's mature canvases. Large radiating flames of color explode over the surface of the image. Although not on the scale of the later color field canvases of Pollock, Rothko, or Still, *The Liver* predicts the invention of the abstract, mural-sized canvas, in which color is designed to envelope our vision and assert its deep, symbolic roots. Abstract Expressionism, which Gorky helped to pioneer, has been described as a movement in which color seduces the viewer into a "regression" toward various "primitive" psychological or mythological states.[8] Although there is no exact code for the meaning of Gorky's colors, his intentions are not all that obscure either. Gorky's drawings of the 1940s came primarily from his outdoor studies of nature. The greens and browns that are peppered through many of his drawings and paintings can be taken at face value as generally suggestive of landscape. However, as Jim Jordan has witnessed, "The summer Virginia landscape is in actual color, despite its other kinds of variety, a most monotonous green. Yet in the drawings of the period green is merely one equivalent color among many."[9] For Gorky, color was primarily emotional, not mimetic. One of the dominant colors in *The Liver*, for example, is red, a traditional reference to blood, fire, and erotic desire. The mood of *The Liver* was apparently no mystery to de Kooning, who told Sidney Janis it was "about women as much as it was about landscape,"[10] a subject with which de Kooning was familiar. Conventional wisdom suggests that de Kooning's famous "Women" evolved into sensuous landscapes of the 1950s and 1970s, one bearing the poignant title *Woman as Landscape*, 1954. As Robert Rosenblum aptly described, "Whether digging for clams, squatting in the water with spread thighs or standing like a giantess emerging from the sea, these de Kooning women, like their counterparts in Picasso, are clumpy carnal creatures, so primordial in their contact with the elements that they swiftly become the stuff of primitive myth — remote deities of earth, sand and water who embody the generative forces of nature."[11] Indeed, de Kooning's appreciation of *The Liver* is based on his understanding of the mytho-erotic possibilities suggested in the painting.

Nonetheless, *The Liver* was not as spontaneously worked over as de Kooning's later works. Rather, its structure was worked out precisely in a detailed drawing of 1943. It is this drawing that establishes *The Liver*'s debt to Miró. Like Miró, Gorky saw drawing as a critical element in painting, articulating through graphic gesture and intricate outlines organic forms that have multiple identities, often erotic in character. Gorky obviously admired Miró's works of the 1920s, which depicted images of his native Spanish landscape. Miró's surreal landscapes, animated with playful erotic references, became an increasingly apparent model for Gorky's works of the 1940s.

Joan Miró, *Carnival of Harlequin*, 1924–25. Oil on canvas, 26 × 36 ⅝ inches. Collection Albright-Knox Art Gallery, Buffalo, New York. Room of Contemporary Art Fund, 1940

The Liver is comparable to Miró's pivotal works *The Tilled Field*, 1923–24, or the *Carnival of Harlequin*, 1924–25, which combine the Spaniard's memories of his native Catalonia with flights of erotic fantasy. *The Carnival* is particularly thick with sexual references: circles with tentacles that suggest spiders or vaginas and flame-like silhouettes that evoke the female body — images that are echoed in *The Liver*. Gorky, who was an avid follower of prominent exhibitions and publications, would have been aware of *The Carnival* from Miró's 1941 retrospective at The Museum of Modern Art, and most likely of Miró's exotic, stream-of-consciousness description of it in a 1939 issue of *Verve*:

> . . . Harlequins of smoke twisting about my entrails . . . stabbing them during
> the period of famine which gave birth to the hallucinations enregistered in
> this picture beautiful flowering of . . . a poppy field noted on the snow of a
> paper throbbing like the throat of a bird at the contact of a woman's sex in
> the form of a spider . . . [and] an enormous influence on my life by the light
> of an oil lamp fine haunches of a woman between the tuft of the guts and the

stem with a flame which throws new images . . . stars crossing the blue space to
pin themselves on the body of my mist which dives into the phosphorescent
Ocean after describing a luminous circle.[12]

The Liver is the Cock's Comb is one of Gorky's most provocative titles and was
likely inspired by such Surrealist prose. On a basic level, the work's imagery
establishes a visual analogy between the body organ and the brilliantly colored
comblike plume of a rooster. *The Liver is the Cock's Comb* is also a play on symbols
and words. The liver is an ancient symbol of the soul or passions of an artist.
The cock, a slang term for penis, is groomed or made ready by the passions of
the liver. Gorky later appended his title with another poem: "The song of the
cardinal, liver, mirrors that have not caught reflection, the aggressively heraldic
branches, the saliva of the hungry man whose face is painted with white chalk."[13]
Harry Rand, who has been the most explicit in his explanations of Gorky's symbolism, sees "the hungry man" in "white chalk" as a clown or jester (or harlequin?) in search of sexual satisfaction. He elaborates on this idea by seeing the
title as a sexual pun. "Cock's Comb," according to Rand, may "refer to a conceit
or vanity. Thus, if we substitute 'dandy' for 'cock's comb' and think of the liver
as the organ of feeling, particularly of intense passion, one possible translation
of the punning title becomes something like: 'Love is the vanity of the penis,' or
more simply, 'Love is lust.'"[14]
   While this reading of the title may very well reflect Gorky's wit, it bypasses a
more poignant symbolic meaning, which would take into account that the cock
is sacrificed in legend to Priapus, an ancient fertility god, who was the protector
of gardens and the insects that inhabited them. Thus, *The Liver* is not simply
about sex but the erotics of an imagined or remembered garden. One of
Gorky's most vivid memories of his childhood is of a garden on his father's
farm:

> My father had a little garden with a few apple trees which had retired from
> giving fruit. There was a ground constantly in shade where grew incalculable
> amounts of wild carrots, and porcupines had made their nests. There was a
> blue rock half buried in the black earth with a few patches of moss placed
> here and there like fallen clouds . . . . This garden was identified as the

Garden of Wish Fulfillment, and I had often seen my mother and other village women opening their bosoms and taking their soft dependent breasts in their hands to rub them on the rock.[15]

For Gorky, the garden — the most intimate incarnation of landscape — evoked a wellspring of emotions, not only related to childhood memories but to eternal questions about creation and growth, often eliciting an increasingly libidinal response from the artist. William Rubin described Gorky's images as an attempt to "recreate the landscape as a theater in which to project his own psychological drama."[16] William Seitz also understood Gorky's work of the 1940s as an imaginary landscape pregnant with emotions. Seitz describes how the conjunction of a new marriage, the dream of a family, and "the return to the bucolic environment he looked back to so nostalgically" seemed to create the promise of the Garden of Wish Fulfillment, while "bringing into focus passages from the works of artists he admired, moments of past emotional experience or points of pain, fear or sexual desire. All these diverse levels and kinds of images joined in his mind the phenomena before him."[17]

Eroticism and fertility are two of the dominant themes in Gorky's images of the 1940s, and *The Liver* is his most dramatic and explicit statement in this regard. Of all of Gorky's paintings, many of them lush with a sensuous biomorphism, *The Liver* is undoubtedly the artist's most sexually charged work. Diane Waldman described *The Liver* simply as an "erotic ecstasy."[18] Other individuals have noted in *The Liver* a narrative of amorous pursuit and seduction. De Kooning apparently imagined it as representing the sexual desire between an artist and his model,[19] while Gorky's Armenian friend Raoul Hague saw "carnal vegetation" and "impassioned movement" in *The Liver*.[20]

It is tempting to read *The Liver*'s "movement" from right to left. On the far right, a tall, insectlike creature with a spiky horned head stands over a palette/easel held up with two thin legs. Janis described this figure as a praying mantis.[21] A favorite insect of the Surrealists, the female mantis was thought to devour its lover or mate after the sexual act: a perfect symbol to project the duality of seduction and threat that was a central element of Surrealist imagery. Janis remembered Elaine de Kooning's description of Gorky's work — "a cruel and opulent sexual imagery"— being partially inspired by this type of reading of Gorky's strange figures.[22]

This part-insect, part-artist standing at the far right in *The Liver* stares toward an ambiguous presence that combines tree and flower forms. A cluster of feathers, a breastlike silhouette, and colored, radiating gestures surround red ovals rimmed with leaves or hair. Between these two figures is a ring of red, enclosing flower petals, flamelike ascensions of orange-red and blue, what de Kooning apparently thought were paint rags scattered on the floor.[23] The central figure holds a clearly delineated sack that is tied tightly at the top to contain its contents. A possible symbol of chastity or virginity, it is placed squarely between the two figurative presences. The left side of the picture depicts a male figure balancing on his right leg (yellow vertical form), with left thigh lifted at an angle to the ground (mustard form outlined with black drawing). Decorated in feathers or flower petals (suggesting the plumed liver of the cock), the figure penetrates the female presence (vertical oval of red, black, and blue) with a distinctly rendered male element. The far left section of the picture concludes with a number of limp tubular forms emerging from cascades of white and blue. Such a sequence describes what de Kooning apparently thought of as an image of courtship and consummation.

The Liver is the antithesis of Marcel Duchamp's infamous mechanico-sexual *Large Glass: The Bride Stripped Bare By Her Bachelors, Even*, 1915–23. Duchamp's attraction to relatively sterile, pseudo-scientific imagery, as opposed to the romantic and sensuous qualities of landscape, set him very much apart from Gorky. Nonetheless, Gorky and his friend, the Chilean Surrealist Roberto Matta, who like Gorky was attracted by biomorphic erotic imagery, were intrigued by Duchamp's "machines." It has been suggested that an earlier painting by Gorky, *Organization*, 1936, and a series of related drawings were inspired by Duchamp's *Large Glass*.[24] *Large Glass*, which Duchamp left unfinished in 1923, offers a rich field for interpretation. Carefully painted and outlined in lead wire on transparent glass panes, the ostensible subject and imagery were of an enigmatic machine that portrayed the courtship of a potential bride and her suitors. Duchamp left extensive notes on the image in a work

Marcel Duchamp, *The Large Glass: The Bride Stripped Bare By Her Bachelors, Even*, 1915–23. Oil and lead wire on glass, 109 ¼ × 69 ⅛ inches. Collection Philadelphia Museum of Art. Bequest of Katherine S. Dreier

Following: Detail, *The Liver is the Cock's Comb*, 1944

he called *Green Box*. Typically, he presented them in fragments and deliberately scrambled them out of order. According to some of these fragments, the machine ran on a mythical fuel called "Love Gasoline," which passed through "filters" into "feeble cylinders" and activated a "desire motor." For Duchamp, it was an allegorical meta-machine. In the top half of the glass, the naked Bride perpetually disrobes herself; in the bottom section, the Bachelors, depicted as empty jackets and uniforms, are perpetually grinding away, signaling their frustration to the woman above them. According to Duchamp's notes, the Bachelors try to indicate their desire for the Bride by concertedly making a Chocolate Grinder turn, so that it grinds out an imaginary milk. This squirts up through the rings, but cannot reach the Bride's half of the glass because of a bar that separates the panes. In essence, the *Large Glass* is an allegory of profane love, as well as a visual analogy to Freud's famous connection between human sexuality and machines.

The Liver, created eight years after *Organization* and at a time when Gorky had rediscovered nature as his essential subject matter, is less an homage than a rebuke to Duchamp's sterile view of human relations in the twentieth century. By contrast, *The Liver* presents landscape as an erotic body through which the artist can express his passionate and romantic vision. Ethel Schwabacher, Gorky's student, longtime friend, and biographer describes Gorky's work as an evolutionary journey from the sexual to the metaphysical:

> Black accents like gashes. . .define a primary conception of a passageway; of the entrance way to [an] area or shape . . . whether these are sexual orifices or portals to a larger body of discernible reality; we are everywhere led to consider the passageway — the gap between reality and reality.[25]

As an adult, Gorky's memories of the garden he knew as a child remained strong, but the ultimate meaning of that garden broadened significantly. His fantasy Garden of Wish Fulfillment was a complex paradise, a spiritual and visceral matrix from which all life and emotion evolved. The closer he looked at nature, and the more detailed his drawings became, the more obvious it was that his nature forms — often resembling female genitalia, seeds, eggs, and phallic forms — were all ancient symbols of fertility. Landscape had become a conjugal field. This comprehension, erotically revealed in *The Liver*, became an important theme in the later "Plow and the Song" series. For Gorky, the plow image constituted more than a springboard for a lyrical abstract shape. It was an emblem of his Armenian childhood, and perhaps more important, a symbol of the basic connection between man and nature, conjuring an image of fertility and growth, an echo of the perception that is celebrated in *The Liver*. By December 1944, he could write to his sister:

> Vartoosh, dear, I have been occupied in drawing the Armenian plows which we used in our Adoian fields near our house. Recall? I have carved one from wood which I will send Karlen. You cannot imagine the fertility of forms that leap from our Armenian plows, the plows our ancestors used for thousands of years of toil and gaiety and hardship and poetry. A plow must be the fitting tombstone for the Armenian man from Khorkom.[26]

The plow was also a conduit for Gorky's sensuous interpretation of nature. He transformed the plow shape into various bodylike, contour forms in such works as *Nude* and *Charred Beloved I*. The plows, like *The Liver* that preceded it, reflect Gorky's meditation on the themes of sex and fertility; the plow prepares the earth for the seed and is thus a symbol of both themes. Mircea Eliade has maintained that the respective rites pertaining to planting, harvests, and the erotic life are so closely related that it is impossible to distinguish between them. He specifically points to the close link established in ancient cultures between woman and vegetation. The result of the shift from hunting to agricultural societies resulted in a shift of spiritual power from the animal world to a realm in which society and nature are mystically connected. As Eliade describes it:

> If the bone and the blood until then represented the essence and the sacrality of life, from then on it is the sperm and the blood that incarnate them. In addition, woman and feminine sacrality are raised to the first rank. Since women played a decisive part in the domestication of plants, they become the owners of the cultivated fields . . . . The soil is assimilated to woman. Later, after the discovery of the plow, agricultural work is assimilated to the sexual act.[27]

Eliade discusses the erotic mystery of vegetation and ritual orgies dedicated to it. While *The Liver* may not describe an orgy, it clearly reflects Gorky's immediate carnal response to nature, as well as an understanding of the ancient roots of Armenian culture.

The Liver combines a beguiling mixture of candor and obliqueness, a characteristic that would be the hallmark of Gorky's best works. He had proven in the 1930s that he could paint convincing, even masterly, representational images, but his letters indicate his belief that resemblance can mimic the formal aspects of things but often neglect their spirit or the emotion of the painter depicting them. For Gorky, nature and his deep memories of its presence in his early years were too precious and complex to relegate to mere resemblance. Through *The Liver*, Gorky engaged nature not simply as something to depict but as an emotional entity far greater than the convention we have come to think of as landscape. While he was looking at landscape, he was painting and thinking about himself.

1. Seymour H. Knox, in conversation with the author, September 27, 1987. Knox and Sidney Janis knew each other for many years and worked together on numerous transactions. Jackson Pollock's *Convergence*, 1952, and Gorky's *The Liver* were both purchased from the Sidney Janis Gallery in New York, and over the years, according to Knox, Janis spoke proudly about both pictures. He was particularly vocal about *The Liver*. Knox felt that this was partly a result of Janis's own enthusiasm, as well as the fact that de Kooning knew the picture well and had praised it on more than one occasion.

2. Letter from Agnes Fielding to the author, June 4, 1994.

3. André Breton, "The Eye-Spring: Arshile Gorky" in *Arshile Gorky* (New York: Julien Levy Gallery, March 1945), n.p.

4. James Johnson Sweeney, "Five American Painters," *Harper's Bazaar* (New York), April 1944, pp. 122, 124.

5. Gail Levin, "Kandinsky and Abstract Expressionism" in Gail Levin and Marianne Lorenz, *Theme and Improvisation: Kandinsky & the American Avant-Garde* (Boston: Bulfinch Press for the Dayton Art Institute, 1992), p. 200.

6. For a helpful understanding of the possible sources for Gorky's work of the 1940s, see Robert Frank Reiff, "A Stylistic Analysis of Arshile Gorky's Art from 1943 to 1948" (Ph.D. dissertation, Columbia University, New York, 1961).

7. Letter to Vartoosh Mooradian, February 9, 1942, in Karlen Mooradian, "A Special Issue on Arshile Gorky" in *Ararat* (New York), Fall 1971, pp. 28-29.

8. See Ann Gibson, "Regression and Color in Abstract Expressionism: Barnett Newman,Mark Rothko and Clyfford Still," *Arts Magazine* (New York), March 1981, pp. 144-53. See also the earlier work by Maurice Merleau-Ponty, *Phenomenology of Perception*, trans. Colin Smith (London: Routledge and Kegan Paul, 1962).

9. Jim M. Jordan, "Arshile Gorky at Crooked Run Farm," *Arts Magazine* (New York), March 1976, p. 103.

10. Sidney Janis, taped conversation with the author, March 9, 1986. According to Janis, de Kooning had mentioned his admiration for the collection at the Albright-Knox Art Gallery and specifically, his appreciation of *The Liver*.

11. Robert Rosenblum, "The Fatal Women of Picasso and de Kooning," *Art News* (New York), October 1985, p. 103.

12. Joan Miró, "Le Carnaval d'Arlequin," *Verve* (Paris), I, 1939; reprinted in William Rubin, *Dada and Surrealist Art* (New York: Harry N. Abrams, Inc., 1968), p. 154.

13. Sidney Janis, *Abstract and Surrealist Art in America* (New York: Reynal and Hitchcock, 1944), p. 120.

14. Harry Rand, *Arshile Gorky: The Implications of Symbols* (Montclair, N.J.: Allenheld, Osmun & Co., Publishers, Inc., and London: George Prior Associated Publishers, Ltd., 1981), p. 183. Reprinted by University of California Press, Berkeley, 1991.

15. Arshile Gorky, Statement for The Museum of Modern Art, New York; reprinted in Ethel K. Schwabacher, *Arshile Gorky* (New York: The Macmillan Company for the Whitney Museum of American Art, 1957), p. 66.

16. William Rubin, "Arshile Gorky: Surrealism and the New American Painting," *Art International* (Lugano), February 25, 1963, p. 31.

17. William C. Seitz, *Arshile Gorky: Paintings, Drawings and Studies* (New York: Arno Press and The Museum of Modern Art, 1972), pp. 28-29.

18. Diane Waldman, "Arshile Gorky: Poet in Paint" in *Arshile Gorky: A Retrospective* (New York: The Solomon R. Guggenheim Museum and Harry N. Abrams, Inc., 1981), p. 53.

19. Sidney Janis, in conversation with the author, March 9, 1986.

20. Letter from Raoul Hague to the author, October 10, 1986.

21. Sidney Janis, in conversation with the author, March 9, 1986.

22. Elaine de Kooning, "Gorky: Painter of His Own Legend," *Art News* (New York), January 1951, p. 65.

23. Sidney Janis, in conversation with the author, March 9, 1986. Interestingly, Janis remembered de Kooning pointing out the artist-and-model seduction scenario along with the detail of the paint rags.

24.Matthew Spender, Catalogue Notes in *Arshile Gorky: Works on Paper* (Venice:The Peggy Guggenheim Collection, 1992), p. 54.

25. Schwabacher, *Arshile Gorky*, p. 131.

26. Letter to Vartoosh Mooradian, December 1944, in *Ararat*, p. 32.

27. Mircea Eliade, *A History of Religious Ideas, Volume I, From the Stone Age to the Eleusinian Mysteries* (Chicago: University of Chicago, 1978), p. 40.

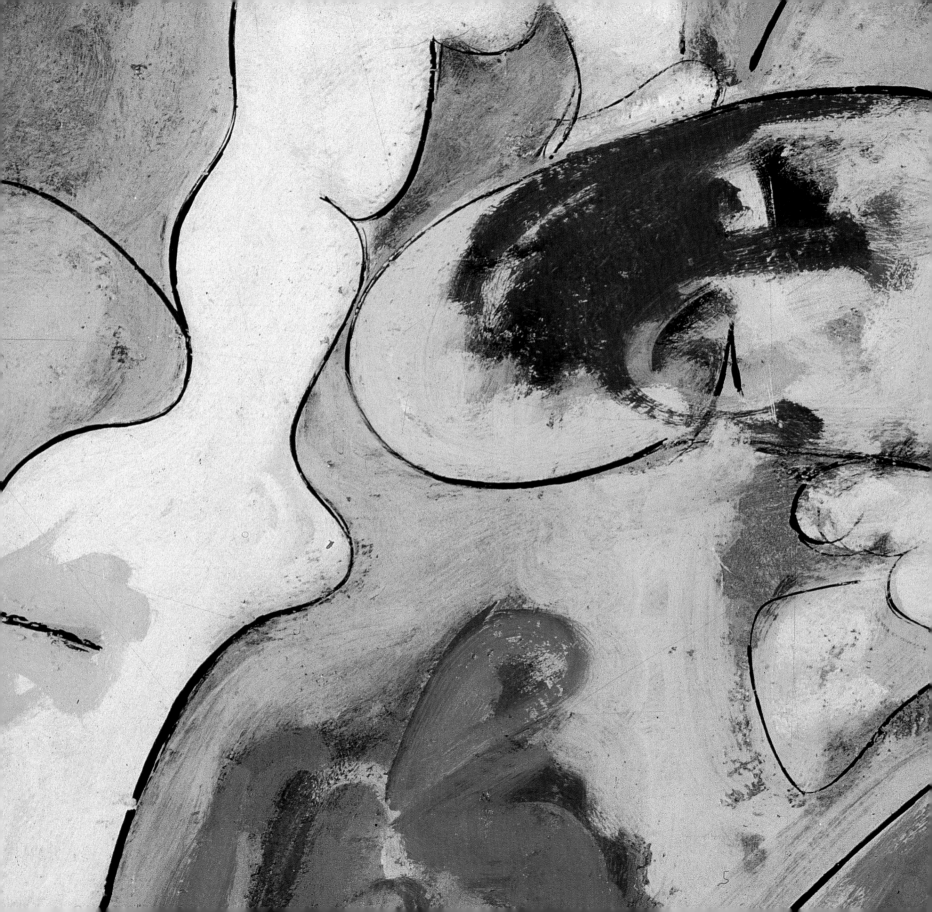

Selected Letters from the Artist

Excerpted from "Letters of Arshile Gorky to Vartoosh, Moorad and Karlen Mooradian," Ararat (New York), Fall 1971, pp. 19–43.

Reprinted with special permission from the Diocese of the Armenian Church of America (Eastern District), Archbishop Khajag Barsamian, Primate, and Ararat, published by the Armenian General Benevolent Union, Saddle Brook, New Jersey.

September 26, 1939, New York City

My beloveds, Vartoosh, Moorad and little Karlen,

I wish that we were together now so that we could speak of the homeland. I long for it exceedingly, especially at this time of year. I have been working day and night. Lately many thoughts have been coming to the fore in my mind. Let me explain, dearest Vartoosh and Moorad, and thereby answer your questions.

Beloveds, some people say art is eternal, that it never changes. Nonsense. Art does change. Man changes. Man changes the world and in the process himself and his art. That is basic to my outlook. It is, I think, objectively true and not merely a subjective attitude.

My dearest ones, the camera has rendered impotent any attempt to compete with it. This has to be accepted as a necessary and a scientific advance. What reason, therefore, remains to sit in the stagnation of realism? Art is more than mere chronicle. It must mirror the intellect and the emotion, for anyone, even a commercial artist or illustrator, can portray realism. The mind's eye in its infinity of radiations and not optical vision of necessity holds the key to truth. It is left for the artist to forge the new metal, to resurrect his ancient role as the uncoverer and interpreter, but never the recorder, of life's secrets. . . .In revealing myself, it is my purpose to reveal people to themselves. An artist must see and feel and understand as opposed to those who merely glimpse but do not really see.

Opposite: Detail, *The Plow and the Song*, 1947. Oil on burlap, 52 1/8 × 64 1/4 inches. Private Collection

November 24, 1940, New York City

My beloved sister Vartoosh,

At this moment I wish that we were all together so that I could kiss and hug all of you. Dearest one, I received your letter in which you asked me certain questions concerning my views on art. I shall answer them as best I can. . . .The artist cannot avoid nature and his return to it should not be equated with primitivism but instead a reevaluation of nature based on the new experiences perceived through the complexity of civilization. It is better to be conscientiously troubled and perplexed by the vastness of the unknown, than content with the little that is known. Civilization knows more about complexity whether or not it has been able to solve the problems of it. And this is the key to the advancement of aesthetic art. Perceiving nature through the eyes of civilization brings to great art more authority and strength. Mastery of complexity involves the experience of complexity. It is this clash of opposites, of new and different ideas and experiences that is so important in advancing great art. That is why, Vartoosh dear, when I speak of the great influence of Armenia on my art, some here mistakenly call it chauvinism. It is decidedly not chauvinism at all and they do not understand. Let me explain why. Vartoosh dear, for good or bad, I believe that I have experienced more than most of my fellow artists. This does not automatically enable me to know more. But it does enable me to respond necessarily to more experiences than they have had the ability to observe directly. As Armenians of Van, Moorad dear and Vartoosh dear, you know well how we were forced to experience with greater intensity and in a shorter time what others can only read about while sitting in comfort. We lived and experienced it. The blood of our people at the hands of the Turks, the massacres and genocide. Our death march, our relatives and dearest friends dying in battle before our eyes. The loss of our homes, the destruction of our country by the Turks, Mother's starvation in my arms. Vartoosh dear, my heart sinks now in even discussing it.

Beloveds, we have been made privy to mankind's evil secrets as well as its glorious achievements. And the living, sensitive, thinking man cannot help but respond with greater than normal intensity. And the remembrance of Armenia's beauty prior to the bloodshed caused by the Turks and their German allies in our land. The art and accomplishments of our unfortunate people. . . .Great art must have as its handmaidens experience, a mind, and the sensitive ability to unify these various ingredients. It can treat the topic in a complex or simple manner, but the topic must reflect the complexity of experience. Some view and cannot understand because in never having experienced they cannot conceptualize complexity.

February 25, 1941, New York City

My most beloved Vartoosh:

I am writing soon because I want to share with you my most recent thoughts. For many days now I have been absorbed completely with memories of our Armenia's Van. Man communicates through his work, but it is also important for an artist to communicate ideas with those who understand and have shared the same experiences and that is the reason I wanted to write of my thoughts of our Van and to share them with you.

I am at work on a picture deriving from an extremely intense recollection of our home on Lake Van. At times I can smell its salt. At times I race to capture the subtleties which attempt to escape me. The dimensionality of our three houses coalesce with red orchards and blue gardens. Visualize painting as the mobile positioning and partitioning of component parts of materiality. Houses built by man's labor and apricot trees by nature's formula and the artist making them all his own by controlling their motion as a conductor leads his orchestra. The rectangular walls with butterchurns and clay baking tools and Armenian rugs pasted on them stretch and twist in seeking contact with wheatfields and cloth trees and Armenian cranes and garden stones, all floating within one another and swept up by the universe's ceaseless momentum just as life-nourishing blood when flowing through the body nudges the artery walls on its journey. The gods before God. The mind before the gods. Before the before. All gently wrapped in the Armenian bouquet of Khorkom, the entire world in miniature and in cosmic greatness, blood-spurting tragedy and sorrow and joy and creativity, life and lifeless, the having-lived and the never-having-lived, the yet-to-live and the never-yet-to-live, full of motion and motionless, all contained within the warm earth and protective mountains of sun-drenched Van, watched with the newly-opened child's eye of your brother.

February 9, 1942, New York City

My beloved sister Vartoosh,

. . .Sweet Vartoosh, loving memories of our garden in Armenia's Khorkom haunt me frequently. Recall Father's garden down the path from our house and the Tree of the Cross upon which the authentic Armenian villagers attached the colorful pennants of their clothing. Within our garden could be found the glorious and living panoply of Armenian nature, so unknown to all yet so in need of being known. Beloved sister, in my art I often draw our garden and recreate its precious greenery and life. Can a son forget the soil which sires him:

Beloveds, the stuff of thought is the seed of the artist. Dreams form the bristles of the artist's brush. And as the eye functions as the brain's sentry, I communicate my most private perceptions through art, my view of the world. In trying to probe beyond the ordinary and the known, I create an inner infinity. I probe within the confines of the finite to create an infinity. Liver. Bones. Living rocks and living plants and animals. Living dreams. Vartoosh dearest, to this I owe my debt to our Armenian art. Its hybrids, its many opposites. The inventions of our folk imagination. These I attempt to capture directly, I mean the folklore and physical beauty of our homeland, in my works.

Vartoosh dearest, drawing is the basis of art. A bad painter cannot draw. But a good drawer can always paint. That is why I tell you to draw as much as you can. Drawing gives the artist the ability to control his line and hand. It develops in him precision of line and touch. This is the path toward masterwork.

Dearest one, I search for new infinities. I paint in series for an important reason. If one painting, Vartoosh dearest, is a window from which I see one infinity, I desire to return to that same window to see other infinities. And to build other windows looking out of known space into limitless regions. Continuously imposing new ideas or changes on one canvas mars the window by fogging it. In elaborating upon the completion of one window or canvas. By that I mean one finite. In doing that I attempt to extract additional unknowns. I place air in my works. They are the windows viewing infinity.

July 1943, Lincoln, Virginia

My most beloved ones,

. . .Vartoosh dear, the series of paintings I spoke about deal with our garden in our Armenia's Khorkom. I named them Garden in Sochi although in actuality I should really name them Garden in Khorkom and I believe I will. For that is what they are. The Americans, alas, are ignorant of Armenia and I have been told that they prefer names of places more "popularly" known. I feel it is wrong and will attend to it. But titles are not so important. What is important is the inspiration of Armenia which guides my painting and which Americans have difficulty understanding. . . .In that series I have, for example, depicted most prominently the beautiful Armenian slippers Father and I used to wear, the ones we purchased in Armenia's Van from the Armenian artists when Uncle Grikor and I rode there by horse. Remember? They insist on calling them Turkish or Persian slippers. Just as they call Arabian coffee Turkish. Beloved sister, you will be happy to know that also included in it are interpretations of Mother's soft

Armenian butterchurn, that pearl in the crown of our hard-working village women. How vividly those days imprint themselves in my heart.

. . .Vartoosh dear, in my works I resemble in many ways our ancient *groghner* for I am rendering in permanency with my mind's eye the tender beauties of immemorial Armenia, as our youthful Armenian days massage my brain and kindle in me the urge to portray our precious sensitivities.

January 26, 1944, New York City

My most beloveds, Moorad, Vartoosh and Karlen,

. . .Recently, I came across an Armenian book with a picture of the Shamiram canal of our Van. Such beauty. Such sensitive beauty. Aesthetic technology. A very human-feeling technology. So different from the soul-less technology here. Irrigation canals are the springs of Armenian civilization and an artist can learn much from them. Their swift lines form antiquity's high fashion. Our forebears hung them like pearl-spray necklaces around mountain throats. Do you remember the Shamiram canal in our homeland?

My beloveds, I view nature in America, but memory plays favorites. And for me, that which we had in Armenia had a distinct essence. Here technology is paramount. And that is not a bad thing if there is human-quality as its basis. But I hunt and search and do not discern the human-quality. Therefore it is difficult for me to accept.

But I am an Armenian and man must be himself. For that reason urban cubism hinders my self-expression for its technological direction is couched in an unfeeling tongue that grates against my ears which are accustomed to different songs. Its lines are straight, but I am a curved line.

My beloveds, one must recognize that an Armenian in America is a strange thing indeed. That for us to contribute to art, we must grasp our experience, understand that it involves the relationship of man to man — happy, sad, melancholy, suffering, beautiful, creative man – and of man to the primordial poetry of nature. Nature which feels in its very unfeelingness.

. . .So I respond to modern life as an Armenian from Van. Man cannot escape the sensibility of his time. The sensibility of his time ultimately gives him the visual language to broaden his ability to orient himself in this world. Any real rounded human who can be impervious to his heritage and not cry a little and not feel very deeply about what he feels as a response to today, is not alive. To be alive is to feel, to be sensitive and above all to be aware. I am very much a live human being. Man creates, is not created.

February 14, 1944, New York City

My most beloved sister Vartoosh,

. . .Dearest ones, my art is therefore a growth art where forms, planes, shapes, memories of Armenia germinate, breathe, expand and contract, multiply and thereby create new paths for exploration. The past, the mind, the present are aesthetically alive and unified and because they cannot rest, are insoluble and inseparable from the future and exist to infinity.

Dearest Vartoosh and Moorad, man should learn to smell with his mind and thereby master yet another of memory's senses. Strange. Recently my mind was seized by the scent of Armenia's apricots, and though of course none are to be found in my studio, I smell them with my head just as surely as I climbed our orchard trees to pick them for Grandfather as his apricot messenger. I touch their softness with my nosetip. Now they float in my work as the humble procreators of delicate beauty. They are the many sunsets dancing silently on the horizon and opening as flower petals to allow Armenian maidens to folk-dance on their warm leaves to the grateful ovation of nature's grand audience. The scent of apricots on our fields.

Dearest ones, my recollections of Armenia open new visions for me. I am using divisions on a two dimensional surface – my canvas – so as to reflect the life pattern that exists in the universe, its tensions, oppositions, actions and counteractions, and to explore the cosmic pattern by the way I move the planes back and forth in all directions to form the complete living unit.

December 1944, New York City

My most beloved sister Vartoosh,

. . .Vartoosh dear, I have been occupied in drawing the Armenian plows which we used in our Adoian fields near our house. Recall? I have carved one from wood which I will send Karlen. You cannot imagine the fertility of forms that leap from our Armenian plows, the plows our ancestors used for thousands of years of toil and gaiety and hardship and poetry. A plow must be the fitting tombstone for the Armenian man from Khorkom. I smell the apricots hot on our orchard trees and they move for me in dance of old. And the songs, our ancient songs of the Armenian people, our suffering people. This I am painting and you will I am sure appreciate it. So many shapes, so many shapes and ideas, a secret treasure to which happily I have been entrusted the key. How your brother does speak.

Our homeland has such beauty. Dearest sister, I completed a work inspired from Mother's apron in our Aikesdan. How well I recall the time that photograph of Mother and myself was taken in Armenia's Van in 1912. The one which we sent to Father in America. And just a short while ago I completed a most successful work emanating from the abstract Armenian shapes of her apron, those designs so pregnant with memories.

. . .Beloved one, Armenia has a warmth and vitality, a strength, a special happiness and pathos. Sad but still unconquered. It is therefore not the world's reflection but the world in its authentic self. At times I succeed in capturing the homeland's colors. At times I fail. But the effort is necessary. To capture on my canvas the rich colors of our fruits. Apricots, peaches, apples, grapes. The rich colors of our plants and vegetation, our grains and flowers. Always I try to duplicate the colors of Armenia in my works.

June 14, 1945, Roxbury, Connecticut

My most beloved sister Vartoosh,

. . .Vartoosh dear, I am working vigorously on many works which deal in truth with our Armenian world. Often I elaborate upon *The Plow and the Song*. O sing of Armenia. I am now in a melancholy way. I think of Akhtamar and the purity of our ancestry's primordial forms. I think of the magnificent brushes of our medieval Toros Roslin and Sarkis Pidzak. I dream of the hushing splendor of Varak and Ejmiadzin. Of Aikesdan's watermill where Mother and I had the wheat ground. Do you recall? Above all my mind is absorbed by the dreaded enchantment of Holy Sign of the Demon Seizer* and the heraldry of its multi-branches, the death masks of its many white faces, the chains which released genius.

Charahan Saurp Nishan (Holy Sign of Demon Seizer) was the vank in Vosdan built by his mother's ancestors in the 5th century. Her family governed it for nearly 1500 years with a dynasty of priests. St. Yeghisheh, author of the history of the Vardanantz, lies buried in it. The clan was affiliated with the Rushdunians and Ardzrunians whose summer residence was Vosdan. Youthful memories of its paintings persisted in Gorky.

June 25, 1945

My most beloved sister Vartoosh, my beloveds,

. . .Beloveds, there are several approaches to art. There are the approaches of the escapers and the approaches of the penetrators. The escapers seek amusement, lightness, entertainment. Sadly, too much of what passes for art in this land is saturated by the approaches of the escapers. Sadly also, but for other reasons, the art of Armenia has always taken on the approaches of the penetrators. We probe deeply, sometimes so deeply that we become sad and melancholy. But the art of the penetrators is more fertile because it seeks and searches and its goal is not amusement but knowledge. Knowledge can hurt in the context of immediacy, but knowledge tempered by experience becomes man's true joy.

February 5, 1946, New York City

My most beloved Vartoosh,

Several days ago I received your very sweet and joyous letter. . . . As for ourselves, we are fine. It is the same old story. Agnes had a serious cold last week, then followed Maro's cold, but both of them have recovered now. And little Natasha is growing and is six months old today. We have taken several Kodak snapshots. When they turn out I shall send them to you.

But Vartoosh dear, a week-and-a-half ago, my studio in Sherman, Connecticut caught fire, as a result of the chimney, and everything burned. I was unable to retrieve a single painting or drawing. The entirety, even my books, burned and reverted to dust. And I would prefer not to write further about this incident, as I don't want you all to worry about it. We are well. And I shall work again. . . .

June 3, 1946

My dearest sister Vartoosh,

. . .Vartoosh dearest, practical or functional drawing is another type. It has two motives, as I see it. One is commercial illustration which is designed for commercial purposes such as advertising. The other is of political motivation such as social realism. I do not oppose the objectives of social realism for I believe that the lot of the peoples must be bettered and that there is a place for such representation to inspire them to help their fellow man. To produce more, work harder, learn better and thereby aid their societies and respective countries. But I disagree with the view that such works as they now exist are aesthetic. I have argued with other artists in New York on that point. I am not opposed to the existence of social realism and much prefer it to commercial illustration. But its existence should not be at the expense of real art. By that I mean that both should have the opportunity to exist and should not attempt to be exclusive because I believe that the two are different areas.

My beloved one, aesthetic or true art is art with depth and feeling. It is the product of a sensitive artist who is expressing his universal feelings for no reason other than the very human desire to communicate his deepest thoughts to his fellow man. It is saturated with thought and must force the viewer to give up a part of himself in order to extract as much as possible out of the particular work.

October 11, 1946

My most beloved sister Vartoosh,

. . .I have three ideas. Beloveds so as to not confuse you let me explain what I mean. In truth, I believe that I am a product of three ideas. The first is *Makrutyun*, the second is *Danjank* and the third is *Hasnutyun*. That is I see my life as an artist as having gone through three main experiences. The first is simplicity, the time of purity. The next is a time of confusion caused from the ordeal of the search for truth. The last is mastering extreme complexity. This last is fruition. And if one understands these three ideas as not being too strictly demarcated, thinks of them as interacting and flowing into one another constantly, then one understands.

. . .Dearest sister, it is difficult to explain such things in letters. I will send you some works and then you will understand better. I weep for Van as Mother wept for me. You understand. In *Hasnutyun,* mastery over complex things does not necessarily require complex structure. It is best at such a time to elevate complexity to that point where economy of line and color express intricacy. When the dancer dances without being there. When nature sings in her silence.

January 17, 1947, New York City

My most beloved and precisious [sic] sister Vartoosh,

. . .The cleverists are not only the money-kissers. There are cleverists among so-called "artists." Truly sad. Beloved ones, Surrealism is academic art under disguise and anti-aesthetic and suspicious of excellence and largely in opposition to modern art. Its claim of liberation is really restrictive because of its narrow rigidity. To its adherents the tradition of art and its quality mean little. They are drunk with psychiatric spontaneity and inexplicable dreams. These Surrealists. These people are interesting to a limited extent. We do not think alike because their views on life differ so much from mine and we are naturally of opposite background. Their ideas are quite strange and somewhat flippant, almost playful. Really they are not as earnest about painting as I should like artists to be. Art must always remain earnest. Perhaps it is because I am an Armenian and they are not. Art must be serious, no sarcasm, comedy. One does not laugh at a loved one.

   . . . The tradition of art is the grand group dance of beauty and pathos in which the many individual centuries join hands in the effort and thereby communicate their particular contributions to the whole event just as in our dances of Van. They can however be rendered inadequate if the linking hands are broken. For this reason I feel that tradition, namely the related ages of the past and present, are so important for art. The soloist can emerge only after having participated in the group dance.

February 17, 1947, New York City

My most beloved ones:

Thank you for your encouraging letter. Let me answer your questions. Vartoosh dear, abstraction is the key factor of the creative imagination of man. It is an experimental inspection of the hitherto unknown which can facilitate an evaluation of it. Let me explain. The universe is infinite, but nature in which man finds himself is, within his recognition at least, finite. It does present him with certain limits. Think of nature as a finite object and all of the plants, animals, rocks, waters, etc. as the cells and skeleton which give it its form and substance. This tangible quality is readily perceived by the human eye. Once so perceived, the human eye is thereby limited by what it can physically see. And so if man is satisfied only with what he sees physically and cannot imagine creatively, he will stagnate.

   Abstraction allows man to see with his mind what he cannot see physically with his eyes. . . . Abstract art enables the artists to perceive beyond the tangible, to extract the infinite out of the finite. It is the emancipator of the mind. It is an exploration into unknown areas.

The Plates

Paintings

1 *Garden in Sochi,* 1941

oil on canvas
44 ¼ × 62 ¼ inches
Collection The Museum of Modern Art, New York.
Purchase Fund and gift of Mr. and Mrs. Wolfgang S. Schwabacher (by exchange)

2 *Waterfall,* 1942–43

oil on canvas
60 × 44 inches
Collection Tate Gallery, London

3 *Cornfield of Health II,* 1944

oil on canvas
30 ⅛ × 37 ¾ inches
Collection The Nelson-Atkins Museum of Art, Kansas City, Missouri.
(Gift of the Friends of Art) F66–23

4 *Good Afternoon, Mrs. Lincoln,* 1944

oil on canvas
30 × 38 inches
Private Collection, courtesy
Allan Stone Gallery, New York

5 *How My Mother's Embroidered Apron Unfolds in My Life,* 1944

oil on canvas
40 × 45 inches
Collection Seattle Art Museum. Gift of Mr. and Mrs. Bagley Wright

6 *The Liver is the Cock's Comb,* 1944

oil on canvas
73¼ × 98 inches
Collection Albright-Knox Art Gallery, Buffalo, New York. Gift of Seymour H. Knox, 1956

7 *Love of the New Gun,* 1944

oil on canvas
30 × 38 inches
The Menil Collection, Houston

8 *One Year the Milkweed,* 1944

oil on canvas
37 × 47 inches
Collection National Gallery of Art, Washington.
Ailsa Mellon Bruce Fund

9 *The Sun, The Dervish in the Tree,* 1944

oil on canvas
35 ¾ × 47 inches
Collection Denise and Andrew Saul

10 *They Will Take My Island,* 1944

oil on canvas
38 × 48 inches
Collection Art Gallery of Ontario, Toronto.
Purchase with assistance from the Volunteer Committee Fund, 1980

11 *Water of the Flowery Mill,* 1944

oil on canvas
42 1/4 × 48 3/4 inches
Collection The Metropolitan Museum of Art, New York. George A. Hearn Fund, 1956

12 *Golden Brown,* ca. 1945

oil on canvas
43 ½ × 56 inches
Collection Washington University Gallery of Art, St. Louis.
University Purchase, Bixby Fund, 1953

13 *Charred Beloved I,* 1946

oil on canvas
58 ½ × 39 ¾ inches
Collection David Geffen, Los Angeles

14 *Agony,* 1947

oil on canvas
40 × 50 ½ inches
Collection The Museum of Modern Art, New York. A. Conger Goodyear Fund

15 *The Beginning,* 1947

oil on canvas

$27\,^{3}/_{4} \times 37\,^{1}/_{2}$ inches

Israel Museum Collection. Gift of Mrs. H. Gates Lloyd, Haverford, Pennsylvania

16 *The Betrothal,* 1947

oil on canvas
50 ⅝ × 39 ¼ inches
Collection Yale University Art Gallery. The Katharine Ordway Collection

17 *The Betrothal I,* 1947

oil on paper on composition board
51 × 40 ¹⁄₁₆ inches
Collection The Museum of Contemporary Art, Los Angeles.
The Rita and Taft Schreiber Collection; Given in loving memory of her husband,
Taft Schreiber, by Rita Schreiber.

18 *The Betrothal II,* 1947

oil on canvas
50 ¾ × 38 inches
Collection Whitney Museum of American Art, New York.
Purchase 50.3

19 *Making the Calendar,* 1947

oil on canvas
34 × 41 inches
Collection Munson-Williams-Proctor Institute, Museum of Art, Utica, New York.
Edward W. Root Bequest

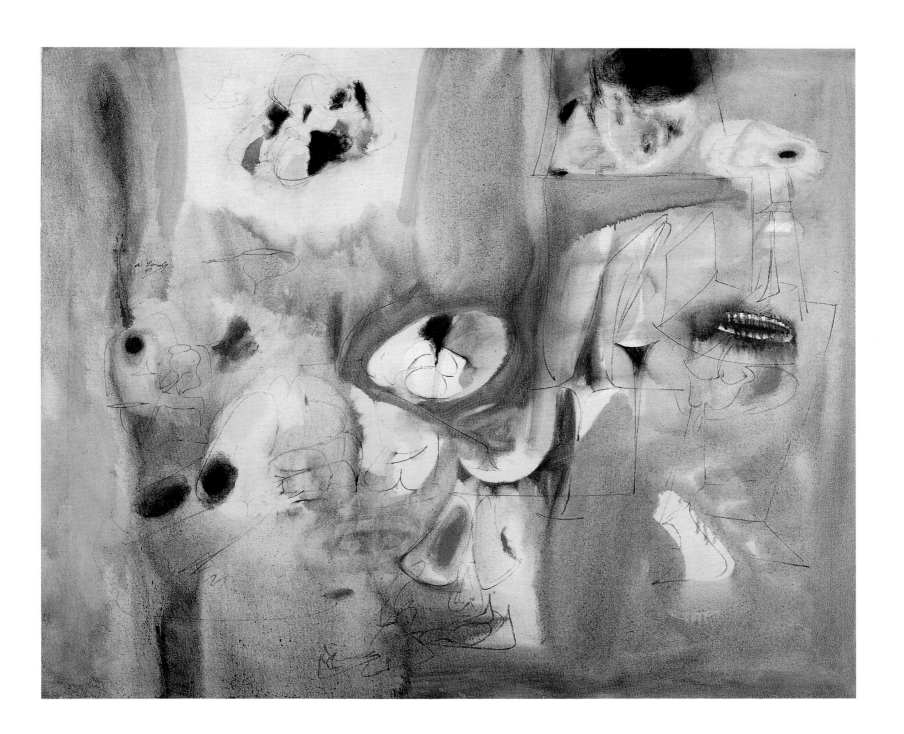

20 *The Plow and the Song,* 1947

oil on burlap
52 ⅛ × 64 ¼ inches
Private Collection

21 *Soft Night,* 1947

oil, India ink, and conte crayon on canvas
38 ⅛ × 50 ⅛ inches
Collection Hirshhorn Museum and Sculpture Garden, Smithsonian Institution.
Joseph H. Hirshhorn Bequest, 1981

22 *Summer Snow,* 1947

oil on canvas
30 × 36 inches
Private Collection, courtesy Robert Miller Gallery

23 *Untitled,* 1943–48

oil on canvas
54 1/2 × 64 1/2 inches
Collection Dallas Museum of Art.
Dallas Art Association Purchase, Contemporary Arts Council Fund

24 *Dark Green Painting,* ca. 1948

oil on canvas
44 ¾ × 56 inches
Courtesy Acquavella Galleries, Inc.

Drawings

25 *Composition II,* 1943

pencil and wax crayon on paper
22 ¾ × 29 inches
Collection Mr. and Mrs. Donald Jonas

26 *Drawing,* 1943

pencil and wax crayon on paper
22 × 27 ¾ inches
Private Collection, courtesy Allan Stone Gallery, New York

27 *Untitled (Study for the Liver is the Cock's Comb)*, 1943

pencil and crayon on paper
20 ¾ × 27 ¹¹/₁₆ inches
Collection Hirshhorn Museum and Sculpture Garden, Smithsonian Institution.
Gift of Joseph H. Hirshhorn, 1966

28 *Untitled,* 1943

wax crayon and pencil on paper
$20 \times 26\frac{3}{4}$ inches
Collection Solomon R. Guggenheim Museum, New York. Gift, Rook McCulloch, 1977

29 *Untitled,* 1943

graphite and colored pencil
20 × 27 ⅛ inches
Colléction Mr. and Mrs. Michael J. Berberian

30 *Untitled,* 1943

pencil and crayon on paper
19 × 25 inches
Collection Robert and Jane Meyerhoff, Phoenix, Maryland

31 *Untitled,* 1943

pencil and wax crayon on paper
18 ⅞ × 24 ¼ inches
Collection The Art Museum, Princeton University. Lent by the Schorr Family Collection

32 *Study for They Will Take My Island,* 1944

wax crayon and pencil on paper
22 × 30 inches
Collection The Brooklyn Museum. Dick S. Ramsay Fund 57.16

33 *Untitled,* 1944

pencil and crayon on paper
19 $^{13}/_{16}$ × 25 $^{7}/_{16}$ inches
Collection Hirshhorn Museum and Sculpture Garden, Smithsonian Institution.
Gift of Joseph H. Hirshhorn, 1966

To my Dear good friend Jeanne

1947   Gorky

34 *Untitled,* 1944

crayon, watercolor, and pencil on paper
19 ¾ × 26 ½ inches
Courtesy C & M Arts, New York

35 *Virginia Landscape,* 1944

pencil and wax crayon on paper
22 × 30 inches
Collection National Gallery of Art, Washington.
Gift (Partial and Promised) of Mrs. Walter Salant,
in Honor of the Fiftieth Anniversary of the National Gallery of Art

36 *Composition II*, 1946

graphite and colored crayon on paper
18 ⅞ × 25 ¼ inches
Collection The Baltimore Museum of Art. Nelson and Juanita Greif Gutman Collection

37 Fireplace in Virginia, 1946

pencil and crayon on paper
21 ¾ × 29 ½ inches
Collection Mr. and Mrs. Stanley R. Gumberg, Pittsburgh

38 *The Plow and the Song,* 1946

pencil, charcoal, crayon, pastel, and oil on paper
47 7/8 × 59 3/8 inches
Collection National Gallery of Art, Washington. Gift of the Avalon Foundation

39 *Study for Summation*, 1946

crayon and pencil on paper
18 ½ × 24 ½ inches
Collection Whitney Museum of American Art, New York.
Gift of Mr. and Mrs. Wolfgang S. Schwabacher, 50.18

40 *Untitled,* 1946

pencil and crayon on paper
12 × 29 inches
Courtesy The John McEnroe Gallery, New York

41 *Virginia — Summer,* 1946

pencil and crayon on paper
$18^{15}/_{16} \times 24\,^{3}/_{8}$ inches
Collection The Museum of Fine Arts, Houston.
Museum purchase with funds provided by Oveta Culp Hobby

42 *The Limit,* 1947

oil on paper mounted on burlap
50 ¾ × 62 ½ inches
Private Collection, on loan to the National Gallery of Art, Washington

Catalogue of the Exhibition

Paintings

1 *Garden in Sochi*, 1941
oil on canvas
44 ¼ × 62 ¼ inches
Collection The Museum of Modern Art, New York. Purchase Fund and gift of
Mr. and Mrs. Wolfgang S. Schwabacher (by exchange)

2 *Waterfall*, 1942–43
oil on canvas
60 × 44 inches
Collection Tate Gallery, London

3 *Cornfield of Health II*, 1944
oil on canvas
30 ⅛ × 37 ¾ inches
Collection The Nelson-Atkins Museum of Art, Kansas City, Missouri
(Gift of the Friends of Art) F66–23

4 *Good Afternoon, Mrs. Lincoln*, 1944
oil on canvas
30 × 38 inches
Private Collection, courtesy Allan Stone Gallery, New York

5 *How My Mother's Embroidered Apron Unfolds in My Life*, 1944
oil on canvas
40 × 45 inches
Collection Seattle Art Museum. Gift of Mr. and Mrs. Bagley Wright

6 *The Liver is the Cock's Comb*, 1944
oil on canvas
73 ¼ × 98 inches
Collection Albright-Knox Art Gallery, Buffalo, New York. Gift of Seymour H.
Knox, 1956

7 *Love of the New Gun*, 1944
oil on canvas
30 × 38 inches
The Menil Collection, Houston

8 *One Year the Milkweed*, 1944
oil on canvas
37 × 47 inches
Collection National Gallery of Art, Washington. Ailsa Mellon Bruce Fund

9 *The Sun, The Dervish in the Tree*, 1944
oil on canvas
35 ¾ × 47 inches
Collection Denise and Andrew Saul

10 *They Will Take My Island*, 1944
oil on canvas
38 × 48 inches
Collection Art Gallery of Ontario, Toronto.
Purchase with assistance from the Volunteer Committee Fund, 1980

11 *Water of the Flowery Mill*, 1944
oil on canvas
42 ¼ × 48 ¾ inches
Collection The Metropolitan Museum of Art, New York. George A. Hearn Fund,
1956

12 *Golden Brown*, ca. 1945
oil on canvas
43 ½ × 56 inches
Collection Washington University Gallery of Art, St. Louis.
University Purchase, Bixby Fund, 1953

13 *Charred Beloved I*, 1946
oil on canvas
58 ½ × 39 ¾ inches
Collection David Geffen, Los Angeles

14 *Agony*, 1947
oil on canvas
40 × 50 ½ inches
Collection The Museum of Modern Art, New York. A. Conger Goodyear Fund

15 *The Beginning*, 1947
oil on canvas
27 ¾ × 37 ½ inches
Israel Museum Collection. Gift of Mrs. H. Gates Lloyd, Haverford, Pennsylvania

16 *The Betrothal*, 1947
oil on canvas
50 ⅝ × 39 ¼ inches
Collection Yale University Art Gallery. The Katharine Ordway Collection

17 *The Betrothal I*, 1947
oil on paper on composition board
51 × 40 1/16 inches
Collection The Museum of Contemporary Art, Los Angeles.
The Rita and Taft Schreiber Collection; Given in loving memory of her husband,
Taft Schreiber, by Rita Schreiber

18 *The Betrothal II*, 1947
oil on canvas
50 3/4 × 38 inches
Collection Whitney Museum of American Art, New York.
Purchase 50.3

19 *Making the Calendar*, 1947
oil on canvas
34 × 41 inches
Collection Munson-Williams-Proctor Institute, Museum of Art, Utica, New York.
Edward W. Root Bequest

20 *The Plow and the Song*, 1947
oil on burlap
52 1/8 × 64 1/4 inches
Private Collection

21 *Soft Night*, 1947
oil, India ink, and conte crayon on canvas
38 1/8 × 50 1/8 inches
Collection Hirshhorn Museum and Sculpture Garden, Smithsonian Institution.
Joseph H. Hirshhorn Bequest, 1981

22 *Summer Snow*, 1947
oil on canvas
30 × 36 inches
Private Collection, courtesy Robert Miller Gallery

23 *Untitled*, 1943–48
oil on canvas
54 1/2 × 64 1/2 inches
Collection Dallas Museum of Art. Dallas Art Association Purchase, Contemporary Arts Council Fund

24 *Dark Green Painting*, ca. 1948
oil on canvas
44 3/4 × 56 inches
Courtesy Acquavella Galleries, Inc.

Drawings

25 *Composition II*, 1943
pencil and wax crayon on paper
22 3/4 × 29 inches
Collection Mr. and Mrs. Donald Jonas

26 *Drawing*, 1943
pencil and wax crayon on paper
22 × 27 3/4 inches
Private Collection, courtesy Allan Stone Gallery, New York

27 *Untitled* (*Study for the Liver is the Cock's Comb*), 1943
pencil and crayon on paper
20 3/4 × 27 11/16 inches
Collection Hirshhorn Museum and Sculpture Garden, Smithsonian Institution.
Gift of Joseph H. Hirshhorn, 1966

28 *Untitled*, 1943
wax crayon and pencil on paper
20 × 26 3/4 inches
Collection Solomon R. Guggenheim Museum, New York. Gift, Rook McCulloch, 1977

29 *Untitled*, 1943
graphite and colored pencil on paper
20 × 27 1/8 inches
Collection Mr. and Mrs. Michael J. Berberian

30 *Untitled*, 1943
pencil and crayon on paper
19 × 25 inches
Collection Robert and Jane Meyerhoff, Phoenix, Maryland

31 *Untitled*, 1943
pencil and wax crayon on paper
18 7/8 × 24 1/4 inches
Collection The Art Museum, Princeton University. Lent by the Schorr Family Collection

32 *Study for They Will Take My Island*, 1944
wax crayon and pencil on paper
22 × 30 inches
Collection The Brooklyn Museum. Dick S. Ramsay Fund 57.16

33 *Untitled*, 1944
pencil and crayon on paper
19 13/16 × 25 7/16 inches
Collection Hirshhorn Museum and Sculpture Garden, Smithsonian Institution.
Gift of Joseph H. Hirshhorn, 1966

34 *Untitled*, 1944
   crayon, watercolor, and pencil on paper
   19 $\frac{3}{4}$ × 26 $\frac{1}{2}$ inches
   Courtesy C & M Arts, New York

35 *Virginia Landscape*, 1944
   pencil and wax crayon on paper
   22 × 30 inches
   Collection National Gallery of Art, Washington.
   Gift (Partial and Promised) of Mrs. Walter Salant,
   in Honor of the Fiftieth Anniversary of the National Gallery of Art

36 *Composition II*, 1946
   graphite and colored crayon on paper
   18 $\frac{7}{8}$ × 25 $\frac{1}{4}$ inches
   Collection The Baltimore Museum of Art. Nelson and Juanita Greif Gutman
   Collection

37 *Fireplace in Virginia*, 1946
   pencil and crayon on paper
   21 $\frac{3}{4}$ x 29 $\frac{1}{2}$ inches
   Collection Mr. and Mrs. Stanley R. Gumberg, Pittsburgh

38 *The Plow and the Song*, 1946
   pencil, charcoal, crayon, pastel, and oil on paper
   47 $\frac{7}{8}$ × 59 $\frac{3}{8}$ inches
   Collection National Gallery of Art, Washington. Gift of the Avalon Foundation

39 *Study for Summation*, 1946
   crayon and pencil on paper
   18 $\frac{1}{2}$ × 24 $\frac{1}{2}$ inches
   Collection Whitney Museum of American Art, New York. Gift of
   Mr. and Mrs. Wolfgang S. Schwabacher, 50.18

40 *Untitled*, 1946
   pencil, and crayon on paper
   12 × 29 inches
   Courtesy The John McEnroe Gallery, New York

41 *Virginia—Summer*, 1946
   pencil and crayon on paper
   18 $\frac{15}{16}$ × 24 $\frac{3}{8}$ inches
   Collection The Museum of Fine Arts, Houston. Museum purchase with funds
   provided by Oveta Culp Hobby

42 *The Limit*, 1947
   oil on paper mounted on burlap
   50 $\frac{3}{4}$ × 62 $\frac{1}{2}$ inches
   Private Collection, on loan to the National Gallery of Art, Washington

Documentation

Prepared by Librarian Kari Horowicz and Assistant Librarian Janice Lurie, Albright-Knox Art Gallery

This exhibition history and bibliography (from 1979 to the present) updates the exhibition histories and bibliographies found in the two seminal works on Arshile Gorky: Jim M. Jordan and Robert Goldwater, *The Paintings of Arshile Gorky: A Critical Catalogue*. New York and London: New York University Press, 1982, pp. 545–76 and Diane Waldman, *Arshile Gorky: 1904–1948: A Retrospective*. New York: The Solomon R. Guggenheim Museum and Harry N. Abrams, Inc., 1981, pp. 268–83.

Selected Bibliography

Archival Material

Archives of American Art, Smithsonian Institution, Washington, D.C. *Arshile Gorky Papers* [includes Whitney Museum of American Art file].

Film

1982   A Cort Productions Film, New York. *Arshile Gorky: A Film Portrait of the Artist*. Written and directed by Charlotte Zwerin. Produced by Courtney Sale. Co-produced by Karen Lindsay. Edited by Carol Hayward. Director of Photography Francis Kenny, 1982.

General Books

1980   Foster, Stephen C. *The Critics of Abstract Expressionism*. Ann Arbor: UMI Research Press, 1980.

   Wilmerding, John. *American Masterpieces from the National Gallery of Art*. New York: Hudson Hills Press, 1980. Reprint, 1988.

1982   Cox, Annette. *Art-as-Politics: The Abstract Expressionist Avant-Garde and Society*. Ann Arbor: UMI Research Press, 1982.

   Matthews, J. H. *Eight Painters: The Surrealist Context*. Syracuse: Syracuse University Press, 1982.

1983   Guilbaut, Serge. *How New York Stole the Idea of Modern Art: Abstract Expressionism and the Cold War*. Translated by Arthur Goldhammer. Chicago and London: The University of Chicago Press, 1983.

Kahan, Mitchell Douglas. "Subjective Currents in American Painting of the 1930s." Ph.D. dissertation, City University of New York, New York, 1983.

Meewis, Dr. Wim. *Iconologie van de Action Painting: Theorie en Werk van een aantal action painters in het ruimer verband van het abstract expressionisme*. Brussels: AWLSK, 1983.

Seitz, William C. *Abstract Expressionist Painting in America*. Cambridge, Massachusetts, and London, England: Harvard University Press for the National Gallery of Art, Washington, D.C., 1983.

1984   Gibson, Ann Eden. *Avant-Garde Magazines as a Guide to Abstract Expressionist Images and Ideas*. Ann Arbor: University Microfilms International, 1984.

1985   Frascina, Francis, ed. *Pollock and After: The Critical Debate*. New York: Harper & Row Publishers, 1985.

   Rosenberg, Harold. *Art and Other Serious Matters*. Chicago and London: The University of Chicago Press, 1985.

1986   Tilly, Andrew. *Erotic Drawings*. New York: Rizzoli International Publications, Inc., 1986.

1988   Kuspit, Donald B. *The New Subjectivism: Art in the 1980s*. Ann Arbor: UMI Research Press/Studies in the Fine Arts: Criticism, 28, 1988. Reprinted from "Arshile Gorky: Images in Support of the Invented Self." In *Abstract Expressionism: The Critical Developments*. Buffalo: Albright-Knox Art Gallery, 1987.

1989   Ashbery, John. *Reported Sightings: Art Chronicles, 1957–1987*. Edited by David Bergman. New York: Alfred A. Knopf, Inc., 1989.

   Landau, Ellen G. *Jackson Pollock*. New York: Harry N. Abrams, Inc., 1989.

   Mackie, Alwynne. *Art/Talk: Theory and Practice in Abstract Expressionism*. New York: Columbia University Press, 1989.

1990   Anfam, David. *Abstract Expressionism*. New York and London: Thames and Hudson, 1990.

   Jones, Caroline A. *Bay Area: Figurative Art: 1950–1965*. Berkeley: University of California Press in association with San Francisco Museum of Modern Art, 1990.

   Paulson, Ronald. *Figure and Abstraction in Contemporary Painting*. New Brunswick and London: Rutgers University Press, 1990.

Ross, Clifford, ed. *Abstract Expressionism: Creators and Critics.* New York: Harry N. Abrams, Inc., 1990.

Shapiro, David and Cecile Shapiro, eds. *Abstract Expressionism: A Critical Record.* Cambridge, England, and New York: Cambridge University Press, 1990.

1991   Polcari, Stephen. *Abstract Expressionism and the Modern Experience.* Cambridge, England, and New York: Cambridge University Press, 1991.

Schjeldahl, Peter. "Arshile Gorky." In *The Hydrogen Jukebox: Selected Writings of Peter Schjeldahl 1978–1990.* Edited by Malin Wilson. Berkeley, Los Angeles, and Oxford: University of California Press, 1991, pp. 76–79.

1992   Kingsley, April. *The Turning Point: The Abstract Expressionists and the Transformation of American Art.* New York: Simon & Schuster, 1992.

1993   Leja, Michael. *Reframing Abstract Expressionism: Subjectivity and Painting in the 1940s.* New Haven and London: Yale University Press, 1993.

General Articles

1978   Rand, Harry. "Notes and Conversations: Jacob Kainen." *Arts Magazine* (New York), Dec. 1978, pp. 135–45.

1979–80   Ashton, Dore. "Forces in New York Painting: 1950–1970." *ArtsCanada* (Toronto), Dec. 1979 – Jan. 1980, pp. 23–25.

1981   Carmean, E.A. Jr. "American Art at Mid-Century: The Sandwiches of the Artist." *October* (Cambridge, Mass.), Spring 1981, pp. 87–101.

1982   Berman, Greta. "Abstractions for Public Spaces, 1935–1943." *Arts Magazine* (New York), June 1982, pp. 81–87.

1984   Vaizey, Marina. "Muses Flee Hitler." *Art and Artists* (Surrey, England), Apr. 1984, pp. 16–18.

1985   Otta, Francisco. "Revelación de lo oculto (Surrealismo Figurativo y Abstracto)." *Atenea* (Concepción, Chile) vol. 452, 1985, pp. 129–33.

Poleskie, Steve. "Art and Flight: Historical Origins to Contemporary Works." *Leonardo* (San Francisco), vol. 18, no. 2, 1985, pp. 69–80.

1986–87   Thaw, Eugene Victor. "The Abstract Expressionists." *Metropolitan Museum of Art Bulletin* (New York), Winter 1986–87, pp. 1–56.

1990   Ashton, Dore. "Roundtrip." *Colóquio Artes* (Lisbon), Mar. 1990, pp. 5–13, 76–78.

Books on the Artist

1962   Rosenberg, Harold. *Arshile Gorky: The Man, The Time, The Idea.* New York: Sheepmeadow Press/Flying Point Books, 1962.

1974   Rand, Harry. "Arshile Gorky's Iconography." Ph.D. dissertation, Harvard University, Cambridge, Massachusetts, 1974.

1977   Reiff, Robert F. "A Stylistic Analysis of Arshile Gorky's Art from 1943–1948." Ph.D. dissertation, Columbia University, New York, 1961. Published by New York: Garland Outstanding Dissertations in the Fine Arts, 1977.

1980   Mooradian, Karlen. *The Many Worlds of Arshile Gorky.* Chicago: Gilgamesh Press, 1980.

1981   Rand, Harry. *Arshile Gorky: The Implications of Symbols.* Montclair, New Jersey: Allenheld, Osmun & Co., Publishers, Inc. and George Prior Associated Publishers, Ltd. Reprinted by Berkeley: University of California Press, 1991.

1982   Jordan, Jim M. and Robert Goldwater. *The Paintings of Arshile Gorky: A Critical Catalogue.* New York: New York University Press, 1982.

Karp, Diane Rosenberg. "Arshile Gorky: The Language of Art." Ph.D. dissertation, University of Pennsylvania, Philadelphia, 1982.

1985   Lader, Melvin P. *Arshile Gorky.* New York: Abbeville Press, 1985.

Articles on the Artist

1979   Suenaga, T. "Mirror of Memory: Gorky's Cruel Change." *Mizue* (Tokyo), Sept. 1979, pp. 5–45.

1980   Fitzgerald, Michael. "Arshile Gorky's 'The Limit'." *Arts Magazine* (New York), Mar. 1980, pp. 110–15.

1981   de Kooning, Willem and Bruce Hooton. "One Who Saw First— Major Gorky Show." *Art/World* (New York) Apr. 18 – May 16, 1981, pp. 1, 4–5.

Kramer, Hilton. "The Case of the Purloined Image." *The New York Times* (New York), June 25, 1981, Sec. C, p. 15.

McConathy, Dale. "Gorky's Garden: The Erotics of Paint." *ArtsCanada* (Toronto), July/Aug. 1981, pp. xvi –3.

Morgan, Stuart. "Becoming Arshile Gorky." *Artscribe* (London), Oct. 1981, pp. 16–23.

1982   Duthy, Robin. "The Investment File: Arshile Gorky." *The Connoisseur* (New York), Jan. 1982, p. 55.

Millard, Charles W. "Arshile Gorky." *Hudson Review* (New York), vol. 35, no. 1, 1982, pp. 105–11.

1983 Avakian, Florence. "Arshile Gorky: A Documentary by Florence Avakian," *Ararat* (New York) Summer 1983, pp. 50–51.

Mooradian, Karlen. "The Wars of Arshile Gorky." *Ararat* (New York), Autumn 1983, pp. 2–16.

Nercessian, Nora. "The Defeat of Arshile Gorky." *Armenian Review* (Boston), Spring 1983, pp. 89–99.

1984 Lader, Melvin P. "Arshile Gorky's 'The Artist *and* His Mother': Further Study of its Evolution, Sources, and Meaning." *Arts Magazine* (New York), Jan. 1984, pp. 96–104.

1985 Beredjiklian, Alexandre. "Arshile Gorky's Immigrant Experience." *Al Manar* (Paris), Aug. 1985.

Rand, Harry. "Great Expectations (of Style)." *Arts Magazine* (New York), Nov. 1985, pp. 58–59.

1986 Barsky, Vivianne. " 'Picasso Head': A Watercolor by Arshile Gorky." *Israel Museum Journal* (Jerusalem), Spring 1986, pp. 99–104.

Rand, Harry. "Gorky in Virginia." *Arts in Virginia* (Richmond), vol. 26, no. 1, 1986, pp. 2–13.

Tashjian, Dickran. "Arshile Gorky's American Script: Ethnicity and Modernism in the Diaspora." *Bucknell Review: A Scholarly Journal of Letters, Arts and Sciences* (Lewisburg, Penna.), vol. 30, no. 1, 1986, pp. 144–61.

1988 Matthews, J. H. "André Breton and Painting: The Case of Arshile Gorky." *Dada/Surrealism* (Iowa City), no. 17, 1988, pp. 36–45.

1989 Matthews, J. H. "André Breton and Painting: The Case of Arshile Gorky." In *André Breton Today.* Edited by Anna Balakian and Rudolf E. Kuenzli. New York: Willis Locker & Owens, 1989, pp. 36–45.

1990 Anfam, David. "Arshile Gorky: Tradition and Identity." *Antique Collector* (London), Feb. 1990, pp. 26–33.

Julius, Muriel. "Unexplained Oblivion: The Work of Frans Hals and Arshile Gorky." *Contemporary Review* (London), Mar. 1990, pp. 153–58.

Hughes, Robert. "Arshile Gorky." In *Nothing if Not Critical: Selected Essays on Art and Artists.* New York: Alfred A. Knopf, Inc. 1990, pp. 220–24.

1993 de Kooning, Elaine. "Gorky: Painter of His Own Legend." In *Elaine de Kooning: The Spirit of Abstract Expressionism: Selected Writings.* New York: George Braziller, 1993, pp. 89–96.

Vogel, Carol. "Gorky Stars as Auctions Resume." *The New York Times* (New York), Nov. 10, 1993, Sec. C, pp. 19, 24.

Selected Exhibitions

One-Artist Exhibitions

1978–79 The Newark Museum, New Jersey. *Murals Without Walls: Arshile Gorky's Aviation Murals Rediscovered*, Nov. 15, 1978 – Mar. 15, 1979. Cat., with texts by Ruth Bowman, Jim M. Jordan, Samuel C. Miller, and Francis V. O'Connor; reprinted texts by Frederick Kiesler and the artist. Traveled to Memorial Art Gallery, University of Rochester, New York, July 1 – Aug. 6, 1979; Hirshhorn Museum and Sculpture Garden, Smithsonian Institution, Washington, D.C.,Oct. 4–Nov. 25, 1979.

"Airport Archaeology." *Art in America* (New York), Jan. 1979, p. 146.

"Gorky's Murals Without Walls: Newark Museum." *Progressive Architecture* (New York), Jan. 1979, pp. 23–24.

"Murals without Walls." *The Newark Museum News Notes* (New Jersey), Nov. 1978, pp. 1–2.

Ashbery, John. "Sweet Arshile, Bless Your Dear Heart." *New York Magazine* (New York), Feb. 5, 1979, pp. 52–53.

Bond, Ralph C. "Murals without Walls." *Artweek* (Oakland, Calif.), May 31, 1980, p. 1.

Hunter, Sam. "Mural, Mural, Behind the Wall." *New Jersey Monthly*, Oct. 1978, pp. 44–47.

Raynor, Vivien. "Art People: Phantom Mural Flies Again." *The New York Times* (New York), Nov. 10, 1978, p. C21.

Russell, John. "Art: Lost Murals of Arshile Gorky." *The New York Times* (New York), Nov. 24, 1978.

Schwartz, E. "Gorky murals: a bit of detective work." *Art News* (New York), Feb. 1979, pp. 136–37.

Shirey, David L. "Gorky's Airport Murals at the Newark Museum." *The New York Times* (New York), June 13, 1982, p. 26.

1979 Xavier Fourcade, Inc., New York, New York. *Arshile Gorky, Important Paintings and Drawings*, Apr. 3 – 28, 1979. Cat.

Gibson, Eric. "Arshile Gorky." *Art International* (Venice), Summer 1979, p. 77.

Kramer, Hilton. "A Rare Gorky and Prints of Prendergast." *The New York Times* (New York), Apr. 13, 1979, pp. C1, C24.

Hirshhorn Museum and Sculpture Garden, Smithsonian Institution, Washington, D.C. *Arshile Gorky: The Hirshhorn Museum and Sculpture Garden Collection,* Oct. 4 – Nov. 25, 1979. Cat., with text by Phyllis Rosenzweig.

"Coup D'Oeil Americain vers L'Europe." *Connaissance des Arts* (Paris), Nov. 1979, p. 56.

Ashton, Dore. "Washington, D.C.: Arshile Gorky." *ArtsCanada* (Toronto), Dec. 1979/Jan. 1980, pp. 79–80.

1981–82   The Solomon R. Guggenheim Museum, New York. *Arshile Gorky: 1904 – 1948: A Retrospective,* Apr. 24 – July 19, 1981. Traveled to Dallas Museum of Fine Arts, Texas, Sept. 11 – Nov. 8; Los Angeles County Museum of Art, California, Dec. 3, 1981 – Feb. 28, 1982 Cat., text by Diane Waldman.

"Arshile Gorky: A Retrospective." *Drawing* (New York), Mar./Apr. 1981, p. 133.

"Prestigious Museum in New York to Feature Gorky Exhibit." *The Armenian Reporter* (Flushing, N.Y.), Jan. 22, 1981, p. [1].

Brach, Paul. "Gorky's Secret Garden." *Art in America* (New York), Oct. 1981, pp. 122–25.

Cavaliere, Barbara. "Possibilities II." *Arts Magazine* (New York), Sept. 1981, pp. 104–08.

Chevrier, Jean-François. "Arshyle Gorky à New York: L'absence, les Odeurs et les Sons." *Le Monde* (Paris), July 1981, p. 17.

Fitzgerald, Michael. "Arshile Gorky." *Arts Magazine* (New York), June 1981, p. 23.

Frank, Elizabeth. "How Arshile Gorky Finally Became Himself." *Art News* (New York), Sept. 1981, pp. 168–70.

Hicks, Emily. "Gorky: The Storyteller." *Artweek* (Oakland, Calif.), Jan. 23, 1982, p. 6.

Hughes, Robert. "The Triumph of Achilles the Bitter: In New York City, A Definitive Arshile Gorky Retrospective." *Time* (New York), May 11, 1981, pp. 80–81.

Ianco - Starrels, Josine. "Variety as Spice of Garabedian." *The Los Angeles Times* (Los Angeles), May 3, 1981, p. 85.

Jodidio, Philip. "Arshile Gorky: An American Artist." *Connaissance des Arts* (Paris), Apr. 1981, pp. 54–59.

Jordan, Jim M. "Gorky at the Guggenheim." *Art Journal* (New York), Fall 1981, pp. 261–65.

Larson, Kay. "The Man Who Would Be Best." *New York* (New York), May 11, 1981, pp. 73–74.

Lawson, Thomas. "Arshile Gorky." *Artforum* (New York), Oct. 1981, pp. 75–76.

Levin, Kim. "Arshile Gorky: Guggenheim Museum." *Flash Art* (Milan), Oct./Nov. 1981, p. 52.

Mills, James. "New York, London Treasure-Troves of Art." *The Sunday Denver Post* (Colorado), May 31, 1981, p. 31.

Monte, James. "The Life and Work of Arshile Gorky." *Museum Magazine* (New York), July/Aug. 1981, pp. 42–47.

Ratcliff, Carter. "Gorky's Search." *The Saturday Review* (New York), Aug. 1981, pp. 66–67.

Russell, John. "Guggenheim Retrospective Charts Arshile Gorky's Passion for Art." *The New York Times* (New York), Apr. 24, 1981, Sec. C, pp. 1, 20.

Schjeldahl, Peter. "Art: The Great Gorky." *The Village Voice* (New York), May 13–19, 1981, p. 101.

Stevens, Mark. "The Great Late Bloomer." *Newsweek* (New York), May 11, 1981, pp. 78–79.

Wilson, William. "Rising from the Tragic with Gorky." *The Los Angeles Times* (California), June 28, 1981, p. 80.

Wolff, Theodore F. "Gorky — Crucial Artist of America's Postwar Era." *The Christian Science Monitor* (Boston), May 13, 1981, p. 18.

Wolff, Theodore F. "The Many Masks of Modern Art." *The Christian Science Monitor* (Boston), May 26, 1981, p. 24.

1984–85   Fundacão Calouste Gulbenkian, Centro de Arte Moderna, José Azeredo Perdigão, Lisbon, Portugal. *Arshile Gorky,* Oct. 24, 1984– closing date unknown. Cat., text by Karlen Mooradian. Traveled to Centre Culturel Portugais, Paris, France, Jan. – Feb., 1985.

Raillard, Georges. "Arshile Gorky." *La Quinzaine Littéraire* (Paris), no. 434, Feb. 16 – 28, 1985, p. 17.

1989–90   Sala de Exposiciones de la Fundación Caja de Pensiones, Madrid, Spain, and Whitechapel Art Gallery, London, England. *Arshile Gorky: 1904–1948,* Oct. 17 – Dec. 23, 1989 (Madrid) and Jan. 19 – Mar. 25, 1990 (London). Cat., texts by John Golding, Robert Storr, Matthew Spender, and Lisa Corrin.

"Drawings of Exhibition" [Arshile Gorky, Whitechapel]. *Drawing* (New York), Jan./Feb. 1990, p. 105.

Anfam, David. "Convulsive Images." *Art International* (Paris), Summer 1990, pp. 100–01.

Beaumont, Mary Rose. "Arshile Gorky: Whitechapel Art Gallery." *Arts Review* (London), Feb. 9, 1990, pp. 70–71.

Burr, James. "Fighting on the Frontiers of Perception." *Apollo* (London), May 1990, pp. 344–45.

Cardinal, Roger. "Resurrecting the Homeland." *Times Literary Supplement* (London), Feb. 9 – 15, 1990, p. 147.

Florez, Elena. "Arshile Gorky." *Goya* (Madrid), Nov./Dec. 1989, pp. 183–84.

Hilton, Tim. "Anguish of an Armenian." *The Guardian* (Manchester, England), Jan. 24, 1990, p. 46.

O'Brien-Twohig, Sarah. "London, Whitechapel Art Gallery: Arshile Gorky 1904–1948." *Burlington Magazine* (London), May 1990, pp. 370–71.

1990   Gerald Peters Gallery, Santa Fe, New Mexico. *Arshile Gorky: Three Decades of Drawings*, Sept. 22 – Oct. 4, 1990. Traveled to Gerald Peters, Dallas, Texas, Oct. 11 – Oct. 31, 1990; John van Doren, New York, New York, Nov. 5 – 21, 1990. Cat., text by Melvin P. Lader.

Heartney, Eleanor. "Gorky Drawings: Gerald Peters; John Van Doren." *Art News* (New York), Nov. 1990, p. 159.

1990–92   Musée Cantonal des Beaux-Arts, Lausanne, Switzerland. *Arshile Gorky: Oeuvres Sur Papier: 1929 – 1947/Arbeiten Auf Papier: 1929–1947*, Sept. 21 – Nov. 11, 1990. Cat., texts by Erika Billeter, Bernard Blistène, Konrad Oberhuber, Matthew Spender, André Breton, and Frank O'Hara. Traveled to Graphische Sammlung Albertina, Vienna, Austria, Jan. 16 – Feb. 27, 1991; Musée Cantini, Marseille, France, Mar. 15 – May 30, 1991; Musée d'Art Moderne de Saint-Etiènne, France, June 20 – Sept. 2, 1991; Schirn Kunsthalle Frankfurt, Sept. 25 – Nov. 10, 1991 (shown in collaboration with the Frankfurter Kunstverein, Frankfurt, Germany); Kunsthalle Bremen, Germany, Nov. 19, 1991 – Jan. 26, 1992.

Piguet, Philippe. "Saint - Etiènne: Arshile Gorky." *L'Oeil* (Lausanne), July/Aug. 1991, p. 79.

Pythoud, Laurence. "Lausanne: Arshile Gorky." *L'Oeil* (Lausanne), Oct. 1990, pp. 88–89.

1991   Louis Newman Galleries, Beverly Hills, California. *Arshile Gorky: Drawings*, Feb.14 – Mar. 5, 1991. Cat.

1992   Peggy Guggenheim Collection, Venice, Italy. *Arshile Gorky: Works on Paper/ Opere su Carta*, Apr. – June 1992. Cat., texts by Thomas

Krens, André Breton, Afro, and Melvin P. Lader. Traveled to Palazzo delle Esposizioni, Rome, Italy, Oct. 14 – Nov. 30, 1992.

D'Alesio, Maria. "Mostre d'arte." *Studi Romani* (Rome), July – Dec. 1992, p. 410.

1993   Galerie Marwan Hoss, Paris, France. *Arshile Gorky, 40 Dessins 1931–1943*, May 12 – July 24, 1993. Cat., text by Yves Michaud.

"Rare: Gorky." *Connaissance des Arts* (Paris), June 1993, p. 26.

Pythoud, Laurence. "Arshile Gorky: 40 Dessins Inédits." *L'Oeil* (Lausanne), June 1993, p. 85.

1993–94   Whitney Museum of American Art, New York, New York. *Collection in Context: Gorky's Betrothals*, Oct. 6, 1993 – Jan. 9, 1994. Brochure, texts by Adam D. Weinberg, Klaus Kertess, and Paul Schimmel.

Cotter, Holland. "Collection in Context: Gorky's Betrothals." *The New York Times* (New York), Dec. 31, 1993, Sec. C, p. 29.

1994   Gagosian Gallery, New York, New York. *Arshile Gorky: Late Paintings*, Jan. 11 – Mar. 5, 1994. Cat., text reprinted interview by Karlen Mooradian with Willem de Kooning.

Kimmelman, Michael. "Arshile Gorky: Late Years of a Tragic Figure." *The New York Times* (New York), Feb. 6, 1994, Sec. 2, p. 31.

Marc de Montebello Fine Art, Inc., New York, New York. *Arshile Gorky: Late Drawings*, Mar. 9 – Apr. 15, 1994.

Selected Group Exhibitions

1979   Munson-Williams-Proctor Institute, Museum of Art, Utica, New York. *Paintings from the William H. Lane Foundation*, Apr. 8 – May 27, 1979.

1979–80   Albright-Knox Art Gallery, Buffalo, New York. *Art for the Vice-President's House From Northeast Museums*, Mar. 6 – 13, 1979. Traveled to Vice-President's House, Washington, D.C., Apr. 1, 1979 – Mar. 31, 1980.

1979–82   The Solomon R. Guggenheim Museum, New York. *Master Drawings and Watercolors of the Nineteenth and Twentieth Centuries*, Aug. 24 – Oct. 7, 1979. Organized by the Baltimore Museum of Art, Maryland, and the American Federation of Arts, New York. Cat., introduction by Victor Carlson; entries by Carol Hynning Smith. Traveled to Des Moines Art Center, Iowa, Nov. 19, 1979–Jan. 6, 1980; The Art Museum of South Texas, Corpus Christi, Feb. 8 – Mar. 16, 1980; The Museum of Fine Arts, Houston, Texas, May 1 – June 22, 1980; Denver Art Museum, Colorado, July 12 – Aug. 24, 1980; The Baltimore Museum of Art, Maryland, Oct. 17 – Nov. 28, 1982.

1980   Maxwell Davidson Gallery, New York, New York. *Around Surrealism*, May 3 – June 14, 1980. Cat.

1980–81   Centre Georges Pompidou, Paris, France. *Les Réalismes: 1919–1939*, Dec. 17, 1980 – Apr. 20, 1981. Cat., texts by Wieland Schmied, Jean Clair, Zeno Birolli, Fanette Roche-Pézard, et al. Traveled to Staatliche Kunsthalle Berlin, May 10 – June 30, 1981.

1981   Nassau County Museum of Fine Art, Roslyn, New York. *The Abstract Expressionists and Their Precursors,* Jan. 17 – Mar. 22, 1981. Cat., texts by Constance Schwartz, Max Kozloff, and Dore Ashton.

1982   Whitney Museum of American Art, New York, New York. *Abstract Drawings 1911–1981: Selections from the Permanent Collection*, May 5 – July 11, 1982. Brochure, text by Paul Cummings.

1982–83   The Solomon R. Guggenheim Museum, New York, New York. *60 Works: The Peggy Guggenheim Collection*, Nov. 18, 1982 – Mar. 13, 1983. Cat., foreword by Thomas M. Messer.

1983   Jeremy Stone Gallery, San Francisco, California. *Willem de Kooning & Arshile Gorky: A Selection of Drawings and Paintings*, Feb. 1 – 26, 1983.

1983–84   Museum of Fine Arts, Boston, Massachusetts. *The Lane Collection: 20th Century Paintings in the American Tradition*, Apr. 13 – Aug. 7, 1983. Cat., texts by Theodore E. Stebbins, Jr. and Carol Troyen. Traveled to San Francisco Museum of Modern Art, California, Oct. 1 – Dec. 1, 1983; Amon Carter Museum of Art, Fort Worth, Texas, Jan. 7 – Mar. 5, 1984.

1984   Center for the Fine Arts, Miami, Florida. *In Quest of Excellence: Civic Pride, Patronage, Connoisseurship*, Jan. 14 – Apr. 22, 1984. Cat., text by Jan van der Marck, with contributions by J. Carter Brown, Sherman E. Lee, Agnes Mongan, and Philippe de Montebello.

     Whitney Museum of American Art, New York, New York. *Reflections of Nature: Flowers in American Art*, Mar. 1 – May 20, 1984. Cat., text by Ella M. Foshay.

     Vassar College Art Gallery, Poughkeepsie, New York. *The Artist's Perception 1948/1984: 1948 Between Art and Political Action/1984 Progress and Access,* Mar. 23 – May 6, 1984. Cat., texts by Alison de Lima Greene and Margia Kramer.

1984–85   Museum of Contemporary Art, Chicago, Illinois. *In the Mind's Eye: Dada and Surrealism*, Dec. 1, 1984 – Jan. 27, 1985. Cat., texts by Dawn Ades, Mary Mathews Gedo, Mary Jane Jacob, Rosalind E. Krauss, Dennis Alan Nawrock, and Lowery Stokes Sims.

1984–86   Munson–Williams-Proctor Institute, Museum of Art, Utica, New York. *Order and Enigma: American Art Between the Two Wars*, Oct. 13 – Dec. 2, 1984. Cat., text by Sarah Clark-Langager. Traveled to Herbert F. Johnson Museum of Art, Cornell University, Ithaca, New York, Feb. 16 – Apr. 7, 1985; Everson Museum of Art, Syracuse,

New York, Apr. 27 – June 16, 1985; Albany Institute of History and Art, July 12 – Sept. 2, 1985; Memorial Art Gallery of the University of Rochester, Sept. 14 – Nov. 3, 1985; Albright-Knox Art Gallery, Buffalo, New York, Jan. 17 – Mar. 2, 1986.

1985   The Art Institute of Chicago, Illinois. *The Mr. & Mrs. Joseph Randall Shapiro Collection*, Feb. 23 – Apr. 14, 1985. Cat., texts by Joseph Randall Shapiro, Katharine Kuh, and Dennis Adrian.

1986   Centre de la Vieille Charité, Marseille, France. *La Planète Affolée: Surréalisme: Dispersion et Influences: 1938 – 1947*, Apr. 12 – June 30, 1986. Cat., texts by Bernard Noël, José Pierre, Georges Raillard, Michel Fauré, Alfredo Cruz-Ramirez, Martica Sawin, Edouard Jaguer, Sarah Wilson, José Vovelle, Peter Shield, Ragnar von Holten, Frantisek Smejkal, Irina Subotc, and Vera Linhartová.

     Hofstra Museum, Emily Lowe Gallery, Hofstra University, Hempstead, New York. *Jung and Abstract Expressionism: The Collective Image Among Individual Voices*, Nov. 2 – Dec. 14, 1986. Cat., text by Terree Grabenhorst-Randall.

     Associated American Artists, New York, New York. *Abstract Expressionist Prints,* Nov. 28 – Dec. 31, 1986. Cat., text by Stephen Long.

1986–87   Arts Club of Chicago, Illinois. *Modern Master Drawings: Forty Years of Collecting at the University of Michigan Museum of Art*, Mar. 31 – Apr. 26, 1986. Organized by the University of Michigan Museum of Art, Ann Arbor. Cat., texts by Hilarie Faberman, Charles H. Sawyer, and Lauren Arnold. Traveled to Grand Rapids Art Museum, Michigan, Sept. 20 – Nov. 2, 1986 and University of Michigan Museum of Art, Feb. 24 – Apr. 5, 1987.

     Newport Harbor Art Museum, Newport Beach, California. *The Interpretive Link: Abstract Surrealism into Abstract Expressionism: Works on Paper 1938 – 1948*, July 16 – Sept. 14, 1986. Cat., texts by Paul Schimmel, Lawrence Alloway, Dore Ashton, Robert C. Hobbs, Philip Leider, Mollie McNickle, and Martica Sawin. Traveled to Whitney Museum of American Art, New York, New York, Nov. 13, 1986 – Jan. 21, 1987 and Walker Art Center, Minneapolis, Minnesota, Feb. 21 – Apr. 19, 1987.

1987   Albright-Knox Art Gallery, Buffalo, New York. *Abstract Expressionism: The Critical Developments*, Sept. 19 – Nov. 29, 1987. Cat., texts by Michael Leja, Marcelin Pleynet, Donald Kuspit, Ann Gibson, Richard Shiff, David Sylvester, Lawrence Alloway, and Michael Auping.

1987–88   The Heckscher Museum, Huntington, New York. *The Artist's Mother: Portraits and Homages*, Nov. 14, 1987 – Jan. 3, 1988. Cat., texts by Barbara Coller, John E. Gedo, and Donald Kuspit. Traveled to National Portrait Gallery, Smithsonian Institution, Washington, D.C., Mar. 26 – June 5, 1988.

1987–89   Fred L. Emerson Gallery, Hamilton College, Clinton, New York. *Progressive Geometric Abstraction in America 1934 – 1955: Selections from the Peter B. Fischer Collection*, Sept. 26 – Nov. 7,

1987. Cat., texts by Harry Holtzman, Susan C. Larsen, and Necia Gelker. Traveled to Mead Art Museum, Amherst College, Massachusetts, Mar. 31 – May 1, 1988; Terra Museum of American Art, Chicago, Illinois, Oct. 1 – Nov. 27, 1988; Fisher Gallery, University of Southern California, Los Angeles, Mar. – Apr. 1989.

1987–90   Albright-Knox Art Gallery, Buffalo, New York. *Intimate Gestures, Realized Visions: Masterworks on Paper from the Collection of the Albright-Knox Art Gallery*, Dec. 12, 1987 – Jan. 31, 1988. Traveled as *Masterworks on Paper from the Albright-Knox Art Gallery* to Allentown Art Museum, Pennsylvania, Mar. 5 – Apr. 24, 1988; Heckscher Museum, Huntington, New York, May 12 – June 26, 1988; Tyler Art Gallery, State University of New York at Oswego, Sept. 7 – Oct. 10, 1988; Arnot Art Museum, Elmira, New York, mid-Oct. – Nov. 1988; The Hyde Collection, Glens Falls, New York, Jan. – mid-Feb. 1990.

1988   Janie C. Lee Master Drawings, New York, New York. *Abstract Expressionist Drawings 1941 – 1955,* Nov. 5 – Dec. 30, 1988. Cat., text by Robert McDaniel.

1989   Associated American Artists, New York, New York. *Modern American and European Prints: 55th Anniversary Exhibition*, Oct. 31 – Dec. 2, 1989. Cat.

1989–90   Lowe Art Museum, University of Miami, Coral Gables, Florida. *Abstract Expressionism: Other Dimensions: An Introduction to Small Scale Painterly Abstraction in America, 1940–1965*, Oct. 26 – Dec. 3, 1989. Organized by the Jane Voorhies Zimmerli Art Museum, The State University of New Jersey, Rutgers. Cat., texts by Jeffrey Wechster, Sam Hunter, Irving Sandler, William Seitz, and Matthew Lee Rohn. Traveled to Terra Museum of American Art, Chicago, Illinois, Jan. 23 – Mar. 11, 1990, and the Jane Voorhees Zimmerli Art Museum, Mar. 25 – June 13, 1990.

1990   Arnold Herstand and Company, New York, New York. *Surrealism: From Paris to New York*, May 12 – Summer 1990. Cat., texts by Martin Friedman and Shane Dunworth.

1991–92   Nassau County Museum of Art, Roslyn Harbor, New York. *Landscape of America: The Hudson River School to Abstract Expressionism*, Nov. 10, 1991 – Feb. 9, 1992. Cat., text by Constance Schwartz.

1991–93   Weatherspoon Art Gallery, University of North Carolina, Greensboro. *American Prints in Black and White, 1900–1950: Selections from the Collection of Reba and Dave Williams*, Apr. 6 – June 1, 1991. Organized by the American Federation of Arts, New York. Cat., *Graphic Excursions: American Prints in Black and White, 1900–1950: Selections from the Collection of Reba and Dave Williams*; texts by Karen F. Beall and David W. Kiehl. Traveled to Columbus Museum, Georgia, June 29 – Aug. 24, 1991; Newark Museum, New Jersey, Sept. 21– Nov. 16, 1991; MacDonald Stewart Art Center, Guelph, Canada, Dec. 14, 1991 – Feb. 8, 1992; Glenbow Museum, Calgary, Canada, Mar. 28 – May 24, 1992; Brunnier Gallery and Museum, Iowa State University, Ames, Aug. 23 – Oct.18, 1992; Heckscher Museum, Huntington, New York, Nov. 7, 1992 – Jan. 10, 1993; Dallas Museum of Art, Texas, Feb. 7 – Apr. 4, 1993.

1992   Whitney Museum of American Art at Equitable Center, New York. *American Masters: Six Artists from the Permanent Collection of the Whitney Museum of American Art*, Jan. 10 – Mar. 18, 1992. Cat., text by Kathleen Monaghan. Traveled to Whitney Museum of American Art, Fairfield County, Stamford, Connecticut, Apr. 17 – June 17, 1992.

1992–93   Montclair Art Museum, New Jersey. *Immigrant Artists from Smibert to the Present,* Dec. 6, 1992 – Mar. 28, 1993. Brochure, text by Janet Cooke.

1993   High Museum of Art, Atlanta, Georgia. *Abstract Expressionism: Works on Paper — Selections from the Metropolitan Museum of Art*, Jan. 26 – Apr. 4, 1993. Organized by the Metropolitan Museum of Art, New York, New York. Cat., text by Lisa Mintz Messinger. Traveled to Metropolitan Museum of Art, May 4 – Sept. 12, 1993.

Jason McCoy, Inc., New York, New York. *Expressive Heads: Including Works by Bacon, Baziotes, Dubuffet, Gorky, Matisse, Moore, Picasso, and Pollock*, May 6 – June 12, 1993. Cat.

Martin-Gropius-Bau, Berlin, Germany. *American Art in the 20th Century: Painting and Sculpture 1913 – 1993*, May 8 – July 25, 1993. Cat., text edited by Christos M. Joachimides and Norman Rosenthal; coordinating editor David Anfam. Traveled to Royal Academy of Arts and Saatchi Gallery, London, Sept. 16 – Dec. 12, 1993.

IBM Gallery of Science and Art, New York, New York. *Highlights from the Vassar College Art Collection*, July 13 – Sept. 11, 1993. Brochure.

Index

PHOTOGRAPH CREDITS